Previous titles by Amanda Viviers:

Capture 30 days of inspiration
Capture 30 days of desperation
Dear Single Self
New Days
Pause
Reset
Embracing Slow
Seeking Clarity

Dear Creative Self, the letter of our life
Copyright © Amanda Viviers 2019

Published in Western Australia all rights reserved. No part of this publication may be reproduced, stored in or introduced into a retrieval system or transmitted, in any form or by any means (electronic, mechanical, photocopying, recording or otherwise), without prior written permission of the author.

All Bible quotations are taken from the Holy Bible, New International Version, The Passion Translation, The Message Version, NRSV, ESV and NLT. Copyright 1973, 2016, 1993, 1989, 2001, 1996.

All enquiries regarding this publication and speaking engagements:
info@amandaviviers.com
www.amandaviviers.com

Public Facebook Page: @amandaviviersperth
Instagram Feed: @amandaviviers

Internal Book Design by: Kellie Book Design
Front Cover Illustration by: Rachelle Dusting
Edited by: Em Hazeldean

Dedicated to

The 3am poets and washing line philosophers.

The half-asleep business owners and the miracle making bookkeepers. To the leaders just having a go and creative makers fielding their next mistake. To the artists looking for their things because they were lost in their heads.

To those who are burdened by the weights of responsibility and the mums desperate for one moment of peace.

To those longing for a clean house if only in their minds. For those who have become parents again to their parents.

May the inspiration be found waiting in the bottomless hope of your coffee cup. A moment of freedom found as you walk the shopping aisle late at night. May your Internet speed be ever flowing and your hearts full of wonder.

Remembering that sometimes the greatest seasons of growth are found in the awakening of imperfection.

God rewrote the text of my life when I
opened the book of my heart to his eyes.

Psalm 18: 24
(The Message)

Contents

Introduction ... i

Emotional Wellbeing ... 1
Reframe The Messages We Send Ourselves ... 3
The Scaffold of Creativity ... 9
Holding Space ... 13
Learning to Say No ... 19

Connection & Collaboration ... 23
Gather the Creatives ... 25
Diversity in Action ... 31
Comparison is a Thief ... 35
The Story Keepers ... 39
Don't Domesticate ... 43

Rest & Sleep ... 47
Doing Nothing ... 49
Turn Off the Computer ... 53
Embrace Silence ... 57
Go To Sleep ... 61

Technology ... 65
Digital Detox ... 67
Unoffendable ... 71
Chase Dreams over Platforms ... 75
Nothing New Under the Sun ... 79

Innovation — 83

Ruminate	85
Collect Memories	89
The Boredom Basket	93
Ask Great Questions	97
Read Widely	101

Pioneering — 105

Be Curious	107
New Eyes	111
Marred By Dust	115
Take More Risks	119
Get Feedback	123

Spirituality and a Sense of Purpose — 129

Nurtured By the Sea	131
Rhythm and Grace	135
Liminal	139
The Sacred Secret Place	143
Epilogue: the letter of our life	147
Dream	151
Acknowledgements	153
Endorsements	154

Introduction

This moment will never come again.

It is irreplaceable.

I'm not sure where you are right now with this book in your hands, but we together are having a conversation. Ideas will collide, opinions will be shared and our collective imagination will bring a moment in time.

We are both on the precipice of change. It is a moment of transformation as our worlds come together. We could be doing anything right now, but somehow, a random set of events has bought us together.

At the same time, at this moment there are crowds of people in foreign places, taking steps towards their future. Some are opening their laptop to begin a manuscript, others are pressing send on an email to a publisher hoping a contract will ensue.

Some people are holding smartphones in their hands consumed with the lives and details of others. Maybe they are binge watching television stories trying to dull the noise of the messages they are sending themselves.

There is a force that sits between us all and it is the power of transformation. I believe this force is the beauty of creativity. My definition of creativity is, "The transaction made through the transference of ideas."

Every creative idea begins somewhere.

Whether it's in a hot shower or birthed on a train platform with the question, "There has to be another way?" Maybe it's out of frustration when an ingredient that is needed cannot be found in our cupboard or a work deadline that looms.

Frustration, desperation, inspiration and collaboration collide, bringing forth something that has never been seen before. Creativity is a powerful force; each and every person uses it daily.

It is the potential to create something from nothing. Creativity is a propeller that creates legacy and conversation and moves us toward the possibilities in our tomorrow.

DEAR CREATIVE SELF

Right now you are imagining the concepts that I am conveying from this formation of letters and words. I am talking to you through this simple vehicle—a collection of paper—and we are creating a conversation, a dalliance together and hopefully, it ignites an encounter.

Every person has a unique DNA that impacts the way that we see the world. The stories, the grief and the betrayals we have all experienced combine to impact the voice we speak into the world.

Whether we realise it or not, our life is a letter. People are reading it every single day. There is a story within our everyday, ordinary lives that plays out upon the pages of history.

This book is a collection of letters that I have written to my creative self. Ones that I have had to dig deep into the layers of difficulty to find, new words that impact the outcomes of creativity in my world.

Each chapter is a layer of story and outcome that has either held me captive, or reformed the way that I live out my ideas, to continually grow in creative capacity.

As well as a letter and a story, I have included a creative date to apply the lessons I have learnt from this layer, to bring freedom into that part of Your story.

I have been a part of the creative industry for over twenty years and across this time I have seen that there are seven spheres that I encounter everyday in my creative process. These spheres profoundly change the way that I speak to my creative self. I have found that great scaffold and creative process within these spheres change my relationship with creativity.

The Spheres of Creative Process

1. Emotional Wellbeing
2. Connection and Collaboration
3. Rest and Sleep
4. Technology
5. Innovation
6. Pioneering
7. Spirituality and a Sense of Purpose

Throughout this book I use historical quotes and scriptures that have been collected across history. These Bible stories have impacted my creative dialogue significantly and have encouraged me with great insight.

I wholeheartedly believe that somebody needs your story, and that creativity has the capacity to bring a great reformation to our world. As we explore the spheres of creative process, your story, my letters and the messages we send ourselves, my prayer is that you would discover a freedom that was prepared for you since the beginning of time.

Your life is a letter that is being read every single day. This narrative is a direct result of the way that we speak to ourselves about creativity and our place on this planet.

INTRODUCTION

You are enough and you have something to say that has never been heard before, simply because it is filtered through the sheer tenacity of your own story.

Let's go on a journey together and find ways to transform the way that we speak to ourselves. In turn, changing the way that we allow our stories to bring great revelation to the people who desperately need them.

Emotional Wellbeing

"space, time and refreshing is an
integral part of the process of reflection."

Reframe The Messages We Send Ourselves

The way that we speak to our creative self shapes and forms a powerful narrative in our creative worlds.

How are you speaking to your creative self?

I was six years old and I was a part of a local theatre show. The lights, audience and creativity coming alive completely took my breath away. I can still smell the dust in the air and the sparkling temptation of the lights.

My mum was an actor and loved the power of a good story. She had just arrived in a small coastal town and was looking for a place to belong.

We went along to an audition and from that moment on, we were in two to three shows a year for the next twenty years. We found belonging in a powerful way. This community impacted my sense of identity and creative prowess.

Celebrations of life transitions, parties and birthdays were shared with our theatre crew. It was this part of my life that bought great story and community to my childhood.

From musicals to plays, I have constantly immersed myself in storytelling. I loved to watch people sing on stage and the way musical theatre compelled people in their imagination and creativity.

The opening night of my first show was one filled with so much excitement and emotion. I was only in Year One at school and my favourite doll accompanied me everywhere I went.

As the curtain rose and the song floated out to the audience, my little heart was beating so fast. I slipped away from my Mum backstage and found the hallowed ground. I can hear the chorus chanting as I remember this memory from over thirty-five years ago.

The makeup table called me and the mirror surrounded by lights shined brighter than a Christmas tree. (Enter angelic choirs) Without anyone noticing I fixed up my makeup, with blue eye shadow on my forehead and red lipstick on my cheeks. I drew all over my face with eyeliner and then slipped back into my position, running onstage to do my part.

I could hear sniggers and laughs throughout the audience but I loved it. I was hooked. There I was made up like a clown—a little blue-eyed show pony—and my heart raced at the conversation between the audience and the creative on stage.

We all have a story from our past that we are telling ourselves. This informs the letters we write to our creative selves. Often we want to walk away from the mess we have created and never remember those dialogues again.

I have found, however, the story that we are telling ourselves today is formed and shaped by the experiences that we have had in the past. This narrative completely changes the way we access our own unique voice and creative identity. It changes the letter that we express to the world. The way that we speak to ourselves colours everything we produce.

The stories that come from our family, our experiences and the moments we have encountered along the way informs our future.

You see, although the first time I went onstage was fun, I had the best night ever; there is another part of that story which impacted me deeply.

As a vulnerable little girl, late at night after the show had finished and the audience had left behind an empty theatre with rubbish thrown across the floor, we waited for the show notes.

The director marched across the room and belittled me in front of the cast. She yelled and screamed, telling me I was a bad little girl. Scolding me with the direction that I should never touch the makeup table and that every person in that theatre was laughing at the fool I made of myself that night.

This formed a letter to my creative self. One that I have had to rewrite over and over so that I could surrender to the beauty of what was destined for my future self.

It is just a story but I still recreate it today in my mind as a forty-something-year-old writer.

The Definition of Narrative;
A spoken or written account of connected events; a story.

There are stories that you are telling yourself today that have come from your lived experience. Our life is a letter that is formed by the way we speak to our creative selves.

There are three parts to every narrative:

Firstly the events that have happened to us. Secondly the impact of those events on and around us, and the story we tell ourselves from those encounters.

What letters from your past are informing your future?

There are a group of letters that I allow to inform my perspective and they were written thousands of years ago. The people who wrote these letters for future

REFRAME THE MESSAGES WE SEND OURSELVES

generations were doctors, community leaders, scholars, shepherds, fishermen and scribes. The words were passed on through generation after generation and they impact the way that we think still in our age today.

I love to read the Bible and discover the letters that other people have written about life, love and purpose. These poignant words written through scripture have impacted my life profoundly, teaching me to reframe the way I speak to my creative self. The application of my faith has impacted the letter of my life greatly.

> For your very lives are our "letters of recommendation", permanently engraved on our hearts, recognized and read by everybody. As a result of our ministry, you are living letters written by Christ, not with ink but by the Spirit of the living God—not carved onto stone tablets but on the tablets of tender hearts. 2 Corinthians 3: 2-3 (The Passion Translation)

There have been moments in my journey as a creative soul when I have had to surrender to the pain of rewriting the letter that has been preserved on my heart to find a new way. I'm not sure what your relationship is with spirituality. It might be cynical, indifferent or you could be sitting with an open heart but I have found the greatest co-creator in rewriting the letters that shape my future has been God.

Each time I learn to listen, surrender and reshape the misinformed narratives, my life grows in capacity. It can be as simple as a half-whispered prayer or reframing our identity with a sense of purpose and passion. My faith informs my future and it also rewrites my past as well.

The letter we write to ourselves about the stories from our past -those words are ones that speak to our future. They are penned from the emotions that hold us from those encounters and they become the stories that we tell ourselves. Pain, betrayal, rejection and bitterness can leave significant marks upon our story and stop us from speaking the truth into our future selves.

There are letters that I am sending myself internally about my personal creativity and its impact on the world. There are stories from your past, like mine, that are impacting your creativity.

Is curiosity a bad thing?

Do I push boundaries that should be left alone?

Is playing the fool a part of my destiny?

Today as you encounter my story through these pages, I am left wondering, what narratives do we both need to change so that we can step into 'the beautiful redemptive' story that is calling us forward?

What are the stories that our families have told us and the stories that God wants to change the narrative around today.

I am praying that God's peace, courage and presence find you captive here in the notes that I have been scribbling as my letter to you.

Dear Creative Self,

This is our one wild, irreplaceable life. Together let's find the words and new ways to grow, develop and change. This is the letter we are writing to our future selves.

I am sorry for the times that I have allowed shame to frame the story I was giving to the world. Those times when I have told you to be quiet and those moments that I played small to stay in the background when I truly had something to say.

This is a day that we together can make a pact to lean into the possibility of growth. Even when I am unsure of what the next journey looks like.

Also to stay connected to others even when people misunderstand my motives. Even when I'm unable to see the end of the path and the places I will go. Even when it feels like a blind journey of transformation and reforming of the language I am speaking to others.

What if the part of the story required is changing the way I speak to myself, and stepping out into the unknown.

Living out a legacy of hope.

Our life together is full of moments of possibility.

This is the sheer courage of truly being authentic to my story and the lessons unfolding along the way.

Lessons are waiting, new ideas are birthing and there is another way.

Yours truly,

Me.

Creative Date

Is there a story from your creative childhood that is coming to you as you read this chapter?

We all have experiences when creativity and identity collide to create letters that we are writing to ourselves about creativity.

Today's creative date is designed to help you sit and write a story from your childhood about creativity.

Explore the highs and lows. Just let the words flow without editing them as you write.

We all have a history of creative expression and these memories can be building blocks on our creative process.

The Scaffold of Creativity

There is a scaffold of routine that my creative self both loathes and loves. I crave the rhythm of an office timetable, the coffee o'clock that ticks and meetings with agendas set by others.

Yet when I lived in that culture year after year, my rebellious, creative self banged on the doors screaming to be let out and explore the wild fields of my mind.

There must be moments of structure in my creative diary and planning, but also huge chunks of space to be open to the spontaneous surrender of dreaming up something new.

We cannot structure creative ideas; they come at the end of a long winding conversation in our minds. Ideas pop into showers and long stints sitting on the toilet.

They visit in the middle of the night and they arrive at the most inopportune times. We need simple systems that help collate our creative pursuits, so that we are free to roam and explore within the structure of its safety.

Each week I create a plan of what is needed for my week. Lately, I have been really strict on my boundaries around work, Social Media and text message notifications.

I need to write lists of what I am working on in a months schedule and then I layer them into my week. I have intentional times of no phone and I keep optional space in my week for creative dates to explore and find new potential.

We need to learn to discipline ourselves in areas of distraction and focus. There are moments when we forget that sometimes creativity is simply showing up day after day after day.

People often ask me how I am so productive in my creativity and honestly there is no short answer. I keep showing up. I sit in a café with my earphones whilst my children are at their activities and I find space to write whenever I can.

I sit with my knitting late at night brainstorming ideas and their application. I talk with friends about my passion and purpose and I discover the sheer terror of trying again and again.

Scaffold is a really important part of this process for my creative self. If I don't discipline myself to actually do the things that I said I would do, then I start to distrust myself.

When we respond to all the present moments in our lives, we constantly live in a space where we meet everyone else's needs rather than work on the important opportunities ahead.

What if you took your schedule from last week and reflected on how much time you spent procrastinating?

What if you took your calendar from the last year and reflected on what worked and what didn't?

Each month I write a short journal in my planner about what worked and what didn't!

I take the time to plan, action and then reflect on the outcomes.

This is a routine of increasing productivity and also creative spaces of the brainstorming process for my life.

What scaffold do you have in your creative pursuits?

It could include a friend that comes alongside your creativity and encourages you with a coffee. It might be setting aside moments each week when you work on your manuscript, painting or craft. We can have full time jobs and still achieve amazing pursuits in our passion projects outside of work hours.

I often create spaces that I hold space for creativity. If you cannot find what you need creatively, maybe its an opportunity for you to create it for others?

The great dreams that lay deep in our hearts don't just happen by themselves. We need to create space and hold space for these things to be birthed. Your creative self needs both structure and space.

When was the last time you gave yourself time to really surrender to the ideas in your heart?

This is why I love routine and the scaffold of creativity.

THE SCAFFOLD OF CREATIVITY

Dear Creative Self,

Find a rhythm. Gather little moments where you show up to the possibility of time and space.

When all you want to do is binge on other ideas from people, like scrolling and television shows, you are going to stop the procrastinating.

You are going to try and set yourself a schedule that includes rest, rather than constantly expecting more from yourself. Rather than getting annoyed when the deadline looms and frustration brings out the pain of discipline.

Thank you for your patience—for dreaming when you are tired and have given so much to others again. Thank you for allowing yourself the space of growth in those times when you couldn't write the lesson, until it was truly learnt in your life.

Scaffold is your friend. It holds you safe in moments of surrender and when you give everything you have.

Build the scaffold that works for you today.

Yours truly,

Me.

Creative Date

Today's date is to pull out a weekly calendar. Draw a weekly schedule for your creativity.

Choose a time each week to plan the coming week's tasks. Set aside just one hour, to plan out the scaffold each week for your creativity. I do this on a Monday morning.

Next find a way to compile all your tasks; it could be a planning app or a program that helps you to project manage your creative pursuits.

Find a spot in your week for creative dates, like the ones listed in this book.

Find a time each day to write for fifteen short minutes. Journal. Release and recalibrate.

Write a morning routine that suits your creative personality.

All of these simple structures will bring a great sense of satisfaction as you move towards your creative goals.

THE SCAFFOLD OF CREATIVITY

Holding Space

Corporate Amanda was hard work!

It feels like a lifetime but it wasn't long ago that I spent all day every day in an office behind a computer, surviving on three to four coffees a day. Stress overwhelmed me, and people pleasing was my superpower.

I struggled as a leader. Let's face it; I had a lot of maturing to do. I needed to let go of the stories from the past that I had been telling myself. I took the time to let go of insecurity, anger issues and a lot of pride.

If my life was a movie, the plotline had success as the main theme—the protagonist was a lonely young adult and busyness became the soundtrack. I had to learn to feel into my own creative self and retrain the messages I was sending myself.

I needed to learn the lessons and wisdom of rest, recalibration, and where I got my sense of identity. I have always felt the places that I enter deeply. I used to protect myself with defence mechanisms that made me a weak leader, but I have learnt to unpack the emotions I am feeling in a new way.

I notice details, smells, people's moods and the echoes in the atmosphere. Sometimes the result of this skinlessness is that I absorb the stress and feeling that is in the atmosphere.

Every person is different, and maybe we describe these feelings with different adjectives but primarily over the many years of working with creative people I have found most of them absorb and create atmosphere. This is the reason why I need to find ways to refresh.

It can be as simple as sometimes moving to a new room, or asking to work outside for the day. Lately, I have been working on the process of creative retreat practice, where I spend time working on my creative craft with others in a regular retreat.

The art of retreating is as simple as moving inward. It is about leaving our everyday lives and desensitising ourselves from the overload. It is gathering with other artisans, writers, painters and poets, to spend the time reflecting on refreshing. It's discovering and admiring new colours, landscapes, listening to sounds that evoke emotions I haven't heard before. Every time I take the time to allow space, it impacts my productivity significantly.

DEAR CREATIVE SELF

When was the last time you took yourself on a creative retreat?

As I began telling you earlier, in a previous life I was a Creative Director and I spent a lot of time working in the event industry. My work took me all over the world, producing and managing events, some of which saw crowds of over 20,000 people.

Coffee became my refuge. I would force my staff to work harder to meet the levels of expectations that I set. This was because I believed the harder you worked, the more significant your success. I wholeheartedly believed that to lean deep into high expectations and excellence meant we'd achieve great results.

My family were hard workers—in fact, in my Mum's retirement, she is working harder than I have ever seen her work before. I sometimes now wonder though, is that because she believes that hard work is the only way?

There is nothing wrong with hard work, but it depends on the cost to those around you. It depends on the stress it brings into your daily environment. It depends on whether it is affecting your productivity and adding anxiety, depression or worry.

As a creative being, I always look for ways to explore my purpose. I am constantly processing what I was designed to bring to this planet. Sometimes in the lead up to the launch of a book, or creative project, I do need to put in the hours and show up to my blank page. It is not about achieving or working hard, it is about the space between. It is the rhythms of grace.

Matthew 11:29 in The Message Paraphrase says it like this:

> *Learn the unforced rhythms of grace. I won't lay anything heavy or ill-fitting on you. Keep company with me, and you'll learn to live freely and lightly.*

Hard work is required. I do need to face my own creative procrastination blocks. I need to own the ways that I am escaping and settle into the possibility of producing. It is also about living in freedom. Living with lightness in our steps.

Are we hustling our way through because of our need for self-worth?

As I have grown, I have learnt what this rhythm of grace looks like. I have unpacked the way I seek validation from others in my creativity.

Motherhood broke me in the best possible way. Through the lives of my two children, I have seen the difference in the way they both creatively express themselves and how they need to find space in very different ways.

We all need fresh perspectives.

We all need times of quiet reflection.

We all need, at some point in our lives, to hold space for ourselves.

Amid a massive project, often one of the best things you can do is take a break, set a timer and have a nap. Our bosses and agents may have deadlines, but space, time and refreshing is an integral part of the process of reflection.

Creativity that is forced often has a false positive reading to it. It looks like art, it smells like art, it tastes like art, but it's not actually changing people's hearts and lives.

Are you holding spaces to decompress?

Is adrenalin, caffeine or stress framing your productivity?

Psalm 119: 45-55 says it this way:

> And I'll stride freely through wide open spaces as I look for your truth and your wisdom; Then I'll tell the world what I find, speak out boldly in public, unembarrassed.

I want to live in wide-open spaces with a rhythm that looks like grace. I want to reframe the power of shame and striving in my life. Let's together reframe the processes that have become a habit in our creativity and find new ways.

Let's rewrite this letter to our creative selves and find ways to hold space and begin again.

Dear Creative Self,

I know you feel tired. I know that there are many other things you would prefer to be doing than to be showing up to this page.

Showing up to this book. Showing up to another idea. Another should. Another change. Another pain point.

Scrolling, drinking coffee and seeking out validation from others is just so much easier. But there is another way. It is a way that will demand your attention and discipline, but it will bring a fresh perspective.

It brings the wide-open spaces that your heart and mind longs for. It opens up perspective that can only be discovered within the depth and heights of a life lived sown.

Take the time to hold space and to breathe. Take the time to create space to hear from God, take the opportunity to find fresh landscapes and perspectives.

Let's re-write the letter of your identity and the impact your words have on the future.

It's time to turn everything off and not answer any of the messages and write to heal.

Discover.

Create.

Explore.

And don't tell anyone. No quick social media post. Just write and explore.

Create space and discover peace again.

Yours truly,

Me.

Creative Date

Set yourself a time this week to go on a creative retreat. It could be for an hour, it could be for an entire day or maybe an overnight stay. Pick up a pencil instead of a screen. Pick up a camera instead of your phone. Grab a book instead of music and allow your heart to be refreshed.

I have a lot of creative retreat tools on my website that ask questions to help you write. (Look out for my personal retreat downloadable magazines on my website designed to help you do this.)

You could also ask a friend to come on this creative date with you.

Start your retreat with this question:

What do I need to do to give myself permission to do?

Learning to Say No

I have a friend and her name is Anne. She is wise, and very safe. She makes me laugh, as often I feel like a 'bull in a china shop', and she is more like a swan gliding through the lake called life.

I met her many, many years ago but it has only been the last few years that I have gotten to know her better. There is this question that she asks me all the time that has completely changed the way I make decisions.

"Amanda, how does it make you feel?"

You see I've always been ashamed of my emotions after I have been told throughout my life that I am too emotional, too loud, too much, too strong, too opinionated and forthright.

And maybe there have been seasons where I have been this and more. But the funny thing I am learning from Anne is this:

The more I ignore my internal emotional temperature (my feelings), the louder my emotions become. Then the more I listen intuitively to my body and how it feels the quieter and more peaceful I become.

I wonder how curious you are about your emotions?

The thing I have learnt lately is that making a decision when listening to my body, when I listen to the small voice within—it is often a quick no for my best yes. This week I have had to say some hard no's. Rather than making decisions out of obligation, I am making decisions out of joy.

The second thing I am learning is when I listen to myself more than others.

When I listen to my body when I am making decisions, my intuitions, my internal emotional gauge grows. It is a confirmation to my mapping system that tells me that listening to myself means I can be trusted. When I listen to my body when I am making decisions, my intuition and ability to listen first and foremost to God and secondly to people grows.

A quick no, for a best yes.

A quick no to obligations for my best yes to my purpose.

A quick no to people for my best yes to my family.

DEAR CREATIVE SELF

A quick no to social media and notifications for my best yes to meditation and prayer.

A quick no to screen scrolling and binge-watching television for my best yes to my writing page.

Next time you have the opportunity to make a decision ask yourself this question:

How does my body feel about this?

Instead of:

What should I do?

These letters that we write to our creative self full of shame and doubt, can really make us respond to requests, that we would normally say no to. Living out of obligation means you are losing the opportunity to say your best yes!

Today is an opportunity to reflect upon the letter that you are writing your creative self in the area of pleasing others. Leaning into the intuitive response from our bodies, that often already know the answer before it has even been asked.

Dear Creative Self,

Our bodies are powerful, they hold emotions safe in places for us to find later. The creaks and tension I find in my body have been left to discover. Our bodies were designed to show us that pain has purpose.

I promise I will learn to sit uncomfortably with the pain found in my body. Allowing feelings to rise and sit with curiosity with what they are teaching me.

Rather than pushing them down, telling you to be quiet. Let them sit higher and allow the discomfort to inform your decisions and not ignore them.

Your body is a gift and it is beautiful and wonderfully made. There are parts of your creativity that sit purposefully in the midst of your emotions and feelings.

Just listen.

Remind yourself of the wisdom found in the depths of our bodies.

Again.

Yours truly,

Me

Creative Date

Today's creative opportunity is to take the time to sit with a guided meditation and feel into those emotions that you have been trying to push away.

To sit and breathe.

Find an app on your phone, or a podcast.

Lay down on carpet or sit in a chair.

Breathe in and out.

Listen to what your body is telling you.

Learn to trust your body, the secret quiet places of revelation that are unique to you and your creative calling.

Pain often refers in our body from other places. It can be from past stories or current realities.

Take the time to let go of the tension banked up in your muscles and release. We cannot ignore symptoms in our own bodies, as they will always accumulate.

What have you been ignoring in your body?

Connection & Collaboration

"Discovering the depths of our own stories without comparison and competition with others, is an important way to unpack our own voice. There are parts of our story that no one else knows about. Secrets hidden in pockets, of roads we have travelled and places we have experienced."

Gather the Creatives

Belonging is one of the cornerstones of humanity. Whether we allow ourselves to feel the longings of being known and let go of the pain that holds us captive to our past, I have found that each of us wants to be known.

The pain of our expectations not being met in the area of relationships can bring significant baggage in the realm of connecting with others. The natural inclination of humanity in response to pain is to pull away from the crowd and to find our own way.

We are bombarded by constant selfies and quotes that tell us to be a "Boss Babe" and to "Find your truth". Every social media engagement, the likes and constant scrolling reinforce the cultural norm that we should not trust those in our circles.

Our society tells us that creativity is a rat race, and we need to shout our mantra louder. Post after click funnel tells us that we need to find "our way through and don't allow anyone close enough to steal your intellectual property".

These are the messages that we feed on daily. Even if you don't subscribe to them, with every scroll, the comparison game again infiltrates our values.

What if there was another way?

I believe that collaboration amongst creative people is rising, and it is founded on encouragement. There are pockets of wholehearted women who are gathering. I have seen beautiful communities within churches, community groups and friendship circles.

I know that many of us have felt the sting of hurt. I believe that there is enough room for everyone, yet I have experienced many burns, betrayals and misunderstandings.

My work has been copied so closely that I have had to reframe the way I speak to myself about the pain I feel.

The creative ride is often a bumpy one, and the thought of collaborating once again after we have been forgotten, misused and misunderstood can be so tiring.

I have found the way to move forward is to gather again with 'the creative'. Call together those who want to find a new way. Trust again, let go of the pain that holds us captive and forgive anyway. We need to flock to like-minded individuals. I am finding strength in the company of values driven people, who are not obsessed with competing.

Nature teaches us the power of groups, and lately I am obsessed with the daily habits of one particular bird. It's a unique creature that is nourished by the ecosystem it thrives within. It is starkly beautiful but imperatively marked by the power of many.

This bird is the flamingo. There are many unique aspects to this bird, but one of the most profound is that it is rarely alone. To be in a flock brings with it the power of a crowd. Many animals on our planet spend their days surrounded by their kind.

> *If one bird foraging in a flock on the ground suddenly takes off, all other birds will take off immediately after, before they even know what's going on. The one who stays behind may be prey. Frans de Waal*

The blaring pink of its feathers is a beacon for predators, so it is safest with a flock of its own. If you dig deeper below a flamingo's top layer, there are black feathers under their wings that are revealed when they are flying together.

Our creative selves are susceptible to predators when we spend too much time alone. There are original colours and flair that are strengthened in each individual when we gather with a flock. This protective group has a role in protecting, feeding, nurturing and nourishing the individual bird.

What does this have to do with us?

I believe the best place to develop your creative self, is in the company of a group of people who care. Many of the creative ideas that have changed our culture arose amid an influential creative circle who were committed to supporting and encouraging one another.

Reframe the way you speak to yourself about other creative people. The more we collaborate and find strength in one another's stories, we learn from one another. I love to see the collective cause that releases inspiration from our collaborations together. I believe this is the creativity that has the potent capacity to can change history.

> *The heartfelt counsel of a friend is as sweet as perfume and incense. Proverbs 27: 9 (NLT)*

If you are finding the aroma of community challenging to manage, maybe you are just hanging around the wrong creative people. I find that the heartfelt counsel of a friend is as sweet as perfume, just like this proverb suggests. Do you have an artistic circle that empowers you?

Flock to those who have your back. Gather the creatives.

A letter to the Hebrews encourages us this way.

> *Let us hold tightly without wavering to the hope we affirm, for*

GATHER THE CREATIVES

God can be trusted to keep his promise. Let us think of ways to motivate one another to acts of love and good works. And let us not neglect our meeting together, as some people do, but encourage one another. Hebrews 10: 22-25 (NIV)

Seek out a group of soul-hearted people who value inclusivity and acceptance. A core of people who believe that encouragement is a powerful way to carve out a new future. When we gather and create safe circles of support, the results are life-changing. Together let's rewrite the letters we have written about creative community.

Dear Creative Self,

I know you are tired from collaborating, competing and comparing.

Let's together step out of the traffic and recalibrate. It is time to forgive those who did not hold safe spaces for you in the past.

Gather again dear one. Forget the pain of the past; release those parts of your heart that are unsure.

Find the softness that surrounds your heart in the beauty of letting go. There is a rhythm that comes with community when we work together and help one another to find our voice. It is important and terrifying at all once.

You need to try again. Let go of past hurts and find like-minded individuals. Continue to give and never lose your voice for the sake of another.

If someone copies your work, just shake it off and begin again. Stop worrying what other people think. Trust someone who creates with integrity and find the stretch in the creative process through collaboration.

Together again.

Yours truly,

Me.

Creative Date

What scares you about collaboration?

Today to start this journey of creativity, I am setting some creative homework to help you process some of your thoughts around community, collaboration and comparison.

Pull out a journal and let's go on a writing journey together.

Here are your reflection questions:
1. If you could describe collaboration with an emoji, which one would it be?
2. Write about a time when people let you down. Allow yourself to be very honest here.
3. Write the names of three people who you would like to get to know more. How does this exercise make you feel?
4. Draw a circle in your journal. If you could invite someone into your inner creative circle, whom would it be?

Diversity in Action

Being different is not popular in an age of mass production. I remember being thirteen and very excited to be going to my first sleepover—a birthday party.

My Mum owned a fabric warehouse, and I made myself some bright pink and blue culottes that were covered in rainbow fish, with a small crop top. The pants were printed in garish colours, and my crop top was quite plain, but I wasn't precisely a crop-top-sized thirteen-year-old.

As I arrived at the party, I realised my fashion choice was way beyond the guns and roses t-shirts, speckled tight denim jeans and the black shoes everyone else was wearing.

There I stood, watching boys and girls diving in the pool, running around having fun and I couldn't have felt more alone. I stood out like a mushroom in a flower patch. The feeling of wanting to creep away and buy the same clothes as everyone else at that party overwhelmed me.

Fast forward nearly thirty years and I still sometimes have these heart palpitations as I walk into a room, discovering I'd missed the fashion memo. We are all so different, yet fashion, online popular culture and comparison compel us to look and sound the same.

As I watch my two children grow, I often smile at their differences. They are growing in the same environment, with the same food, same biological parents and upbringing, yet are poles apart in the way that they react to situations.

Our current education system really confines people into boxes and struggles to cope with this essential idea in humanity that we are all different. We bleed the same colour, but we express our emotions, insights and companionships with our own individual flair. Cultural impact changes the way we react in every situation, and the Internet has blurred all our opinions on minute things.

We are bringing up a generation of children who are forgetting that the colour of our eyes, the shape of our fingerprints and the stories we hold in our hearts vary dramatically.

How can we describe our difference positively?

Every member of our families is different, and the experiences we have all travelled carry various wounds. The way that I have discovered power is through finding my own voice.

Discovering the depths of our own stories without comparison and competition with others, is an important way to unpack our own voice. There are parts of our story that no one else knows about. Secrets hidden in pockets, of roads we have travelled and places we have experienced.

We all have had times when people have let us down; hurting us, forgetting us and speaking words that are somewhat true but not the whole picture. We each have stories from our childhoods that can remain dormant and we remain wounded, or we can find ways to express them to find healing and discovery.

Perspective and power walk hand in hand. When we find perspective and insight about ourselves, we see potential in the future for growth, capacity and the fulfilment of dreams.

That is why I am so passionate about the power of writing to help find release. Each time we sit with a journal, we gain clarity and perspective about our own story. Even if it's a rant, we are releasing the anger that has been held captive in the story that we are telling ourselves about what happened.

How comfortable are you in sitting apart from the crowd?

Each and every time we discover our own sense of self within the depth and beauty of humanity, it results in a growth of capacity to understand our values. Finding our unique voice is a powerful tool for self reflection.

Our unique capacity to be able to process stories in different ways is the possibility that we all have to live a life of complete surrender to growth.

We grow when we gain insight. Each time we understand our own personal strengths and weaknesses, quirks and personality differences, is an opportunity for us to understand ourselves more. It is the place where we discover and get to know ourselves better.

Colossians was a letter written to a group of people who were trying to work out how to get along. Chapter one, verses sixteen and seventeen explores the brilliance and difficulty of diversity in action.

> So spacious is he, so roomy, that everything of God finds its proper place in him without crowding. Not only that but all the broken and dislocated pieces of the universe, people and things, animals and atoms, get properly fixed and fit together in vibrant harmonies. Col 1: 16-17 (MSG)

We are all unique. Our children are exceptional, their potential is unique—the power of understanding this can shift our need to compare ourselves with others, emancipating us into a place of freedom.

We were not born to be like everyone else. There is a part of our story collectively that is impacted by the discovery of our own unique place to play within it. Celebrate diversity in action. This letter we have written from our own stories and experiences shapes our creativity.

Dear Creative Self,

You are fearfully and wonderfully made. Before the earth was formed, God knew you. He created you and he formed you.

You hands are uniquely yours. With each fingerprint defined just for you. There may be millions of people on this planet, but no one has the same print as you.

Your eyes are completely your own. They have seen and discovered many different explorations that no other eye has seen the same way.

Your stories held captive in the vault of your heart and experience are unique to only you. No one has walked the same steps, or heard the same words as you have. Every single day is different, with new experiences to be held.

You are the compilation of a million stories that remain unheard.

You are brilliant and kind.

You are purposed and full of capacity.

You are like none other.

Made in the image of an amazing creative being.

Keep discovering the intricacies that make you smile.

Yours truly,

Me

Creative Date

Recently I saw my son draw a self-portrait. It was one of the most defining moments in my motherhood journey. For many reasons, I straightaway saw, how he sees.

My task for you today is this...

Draw a simple self-portrait. It doesn't need to be fancy. It can be a stick figure drawing or a representation of you. You can cut out magazine pictures or use crayons.

Alongside the side of the self-portrait now write a list of things that make you different to everyone else. Things that are unique to you, like your strengths, quirks and secrets.

Comparison is a Thief

A thief is holding many of us captive. We are locked in a room that held for ransom. It is a very silent, sneaky, shame-filled part of our modern worlds. It can trip us up at any unsuspecting moment.

We're held captive during a quick flick through the newspaper, a little read of a magazine, a scroll through a Social Media feed, maybe even while you read my stories here in this book.

The thief's name is comparison, and it kidnaps us all at some point in our lives. Holding us for ransom until we find the bounty of perspective once again.

The thief whispers, 'Look at her life, she has it all together.'

It taunts us with, 'What if she actually knew what I thought of her?'

Finishing with, 'If only I had what she has, then everything would be so different.'

> How much time he gains who does not look to see what his neighbour says or does or thinks, but only at what he does himself, to make it just and holy. Marcus Aurelius

Creative people are often caught in the trap of believing that if only they had a different set of circumstances, then they too would achieve what someone else is. These are some of the things I have been reminding myself about social media lately:

1. Social Networking sites are a tiny part of my life, and I will not give them more space than they deserve.
2. Online spaces do not replace face-to-face connection with my community.
3. When online I am determined to encourage as many people online as possible, because many people I encounter are really discouraged.
4. Vulnerability does not equal authenticity, and the people we should be most vulnerable to should not be the crowd, but those under our own roof.
5. Social media is a massive time and creativity drain. Rather than scrolling for entertainment, what if I

did something with my hands and created.
6. I am determined to believe the best about the people I choose to follow online. If I decide to follow them, I will find the best and not sit in the seat of the cynic. Believing the best is a fantastic seat to sit in rather than assuming the worst. Our assumptions about others impact our hearts the most.

> *Do nothing from rivalry or conceit, but in humility, count others more significant than yourselves. Philippians 2:3 (NIV)*

Comparison steals the joy of our everyday moments. Competing with our neighbour is like climbing a ladder that ends up nowhere. The problem is that we have missed the amazing view that is surrounding us. We lose perspective of the beauty that is very present.

Take time today to remove yourself from the place where comparison robs you of your joy. Maybe it's a particular person that you follow on social media. The answer for you in this season might be to unfollow them.

We need to be ruthless in the self-talk we have in this area of comparison. Often the breeding ground of this part of our lives is the messages that we send to ourselves. These letters we have written to ourselves are penned with the shadow of another's creativity.

When we reframe our internal conversations, we need to remind our creative selves of the beauty in our season for today. We need to spend time looking for inspiration in the very ordinary moments of our days. Reminding our creative selves that we are wonderfully made.

Dear Creative Self,

Thank you for the beauty and simplicity of the gifts you have given. Moments when we have danced together in the midst of a new idea, the colours we have created when we did something hard.

Thank you for those moments of deep authenticity, when we found an idea from our own story, rather than another's.

For those days that we said we would not compare our story today with someone else's season.

Let's commit to the stories that come from our own path, not the path of another.

Together let's learn for tomorrow.

Yours truly,

Me

Creative Date

Today's goal is to unfollow a heap of people on social media that you are comparing yourself to.

This is not a blame game and I know for some people this can be really confronting, especially if you find it difficult not to be pleasing people, but sometimes just ripping the Band-Aid off and unfollowing a heap of people is a massive release in the whole area of comparison.

Putting some limits around what you see from certain people really helps to reframe the everyday places where comparison and competition creep in.

The Story Keepers

Through the night, the wind kept waking me as a storm swept past the bay. I tossed and turned, falling asleep and then another bang, shudder or howl would wake me. I wondered if the rain would leak under the front door, soaking our jarrah floorboards. Worry came knocking around 2am that the flu that has been hanging in the shadows of my home would settle in to stay.

I stood at the sink today and saw that the passionfruit plant that had taken months to climb up slowly covering the unfinished fence had died, when nobody was looking. I picked up the tea towel off my oven and I stopped mid air and remembered her house.

This year we packed up my Grandmothers house, after many decades of her living close by, and she went reluctantly to a nursing home. Her things were divided between family members and honestly, I wasn't that interested in her belongings, I'd prefer to hold her hand. A box of things, however, was placed on the back seat of my car and my favourite—over all the antiques, jewellery and letters—were her old linen tea towels.

Each time I hold them, I think of the carrot cakes she would bake and the Christmas cookies that no one has managed yet to replicate. My grandmother is old farm stock and I'm sure these pieces of cloth have been held whilst she watched the news on days when history was smashed open and also the days when baked fish was on the menu for dinner.

Story keeping, cloths that have held memories through my family history.

Story seekers, of hearts questioning as they went about daily life with menial tasks.

Story capsules, of the people calling to chat with her on the phone and gossip about that irritating neighbour.

There are moments of our ordinary days that no one will ever see. There are times when words become powerful carriers of emotion and change. When we realise that the stories laden in the processing of our days are the economy of legacy and hope.

Lately, I have been really off Instagram, Social Media and the hungry machine of content creation. I have been reminding myself of the power and beauty of creativity and story, to leave a legacy that remains.

We are the story keepers, shapers and holders.

Robyn McKee says it this way:

> Storytelling is the most powerful way to put ideas into the world today.

If you look across history, human wisdom and tenacity has been recorded through story. I strongly believe that somebody needs your story. The highs, the lows, the in-betweens and the not enough yet.

As we begin to find ways to allow writing to heal, when we show up to our blank pages and work through our stories to find clarity, hope and courage, God brings strength in these places.

Human beings are shaped by stories.

We find encouragement through stories.

We leave lessons for those coming behind with stories.

We were born into a story from the narrative of our parents.

We live in the story that we are telling ourselves.

There is a story in the Bible that talks about legacy in the midst of our current story and narrative. Joel was an amazing scholar and prophet, a man of wisdom to his local community. He wrote this:

> Tell it to your children, and let your children tell it to their children, and their children to the next generation. Joel 1:3 (NIV)

I wonder what stories will be told to our children's children about the tone and tenure of our current novel in history. What will be retold about this symphony of peace and chaos, an era of change and technology, ignorance and platforms?

What letters are we writing as inheritance?

We are the story keepers, the culture changers and the life legacy leavers. As we dig deep into our places of freedom and hope, we unveil the beauty of discovering and wisdom for those who sit alongside. Further more, we leave a trail of inspiration for those who follow behind us.

Dear Creative Self,

There are stories that you see, that no one else notices. Sign posts towards inspiration and hope. You also see these moments of fear and deep unsure revelations of the toxicity around us.

Thank you for being my story keeper. Reminding me of moments that I would have just forgotten. Looking with new eyes, upon vistas of beauty.

Possibility beckons in moments of simplicity. When our creative voices combine together to look into windows of memory and moment.

Together let's bring forth inspiration and story that leave clues for those following behind. Crumbs of manna, that led us all home.

Pictures taken with our minds and little souvenirs of tasting and seeing that God was present through it all.

He is like a shepherd guiding us through.

He sneaks us behind gates and fortresses, to reveal hidden treasures of grace.

Keep holding those memories and moments.

Help me to write, explore and discover again.

Yours truly,

Me

Creative Date

Today your exercise is to grab an old journal and look through the pages to find highs and lows from past stories.

List out the main themes that are found in your pages of writing. See them as pastures of grace, reminding you of stories now resolved or open awaiting revelation.

Write lists from your writing. Encapsulating the stories of shadows and blind spots from past circumstances.

Read, gather and graze upon the musings of your past.

What wisdom is found in these trenches?

What difficulties now have past?

What are you thankful for?

Take the time to write and discover the stories that now are informing your present moment.

Don't Domesticate

The humidity was so thick, and I didn't know whether I was breathing in air or soup. I was in a jungle, north of Thailand on a slow boat. We were visiting an elephant sanctuary, where we were told that these giants of nature were being rehabilitated from their farming history.

As we came closer to the sanctuary, the smell was overwhelming and the heat steamed off the ground. I'd never seen an elephant in the wild and my expectations for that day quickly dissipated. I saw the elephant trainer slapping this beautiful creature, asking it to bow to him. They were getting ready for another round of tourists to step on up and pay them some money.

The domestication of this beautiful male elephant could not have been in starker contrast, to the group of wild elephants playing around in the trees, that we saw when we moved through the jungle. I sat on top of his beautiful leathery skin, and I realised the reality of the difference between domestication and the call of the wild.

It was a memory I will never forget. Animals are designed to live without borders. They were created by a Designer who made an environment within the world for them to roam about with freedom.

How free do you feel to explore the wildness of the environments that you are grazing in?

> *He has filled them with the skill to do all kinds of work*
> *as engravers, designers, embroiderers in blue, purple*
> *and scarlet yarn and fine linen, and weavers—all of them*
> *skilled workers and designers. Exodus 35: 35 (NIV)*

I have come to see that creative people are domesticated all the time. The call of the wild inside the hearts and lives of those who lean towards pioneering, is a strong, wielding power.

Leaders trying to maintain creative control over their teams often control this creative force. They can be found drawing boundaries around idea generation by their teams, in the name of productivity.

DEAR CREATIVE SELF

After more than twenty-five years of leading and mentoring creative people, I have come to realise that there is no formula for productivity that fits a large group of people.

Yes, there are different practises that help individuals to find their voice and flow. But when we try to domesticate the ideas and creativity of individuals, we lose the potency of the force that was designed to break the status quo.

To domesticate is to call people into line, fit them into the nine-to-five—you know the daily grind. Creative ideas that break culture, identities and bring change do not come on demand. You cannot turn on creativity like a tap or a television stream.

Ideas are not like instant coffee that can be released from a jar from your cupboard. They are like the brewing of kombucha, that needs the right temperature, ingredients, and still the flavour may need more time to develop.

When productivity becomes the leading indicator of creativity, we have a domesticating problem. I am not talking about a life without any rules for creative people, so they live with no convention or moral compass for right and wrong. I am talking about the way that we expect creative industry professionals to produce on command.

This is the domestication of the creative mind. To bring out the best in your creative self, it is imperative that you have spaces and places that allow you to move, perceive and collect data to help bring forth something new.

It is the difference between stock imagery that has been filtered and overly staged, in comparison to an idea that has never been seen before, coming from a place of deep inspiration.

Creativity takes time.

It is wild.

It's a force that needs free, open spaces to be unveiled.

A new expression or song cannot be planned. I am not talking about someone who sleeps in, is lazy and is not willing to be responsible for his or her own tasks. I am talking about the time required to process the depths of an uncommon idea.

These kinds of ideas cost the creative soul. They are late night, early morning and flooding of ideas that come at the most inconvenient of times.

Don't domesticate the creativity that is brewing deep within you. It may seem easy to take the short cut, to toe the line and to copy what someone else is doing. Instead, find a way to come back to yourself. Do the work to unpack the prism that only your eyes have been designed to see.

There is enough clip art, stock images and plagiarism in the world. Find a way to discover the voice that is deeply embedded within your own heart and story. Dig deep into the fullness of who you are designed to become. Rewriting this letter to our creative selves is a powerful practise of showing up again and again to our blank pages.

Dear Creative Self,

I am thankful for the times you have been spontaneous with your ideas.

There is a depth of courage with the release of a new idea and thankyou for the times that you have enabled insight to help me see new ways.

Let's remember to hang out with people who are not playing it safe, but pioneering again. I release any domestication of my inner being to fit other people's view of what I should be doing.

Help me to celebrate and empower my wild ideas.

Yours truly,

Me

Creative Date

Write a list of ways that you are domesticating your creativity to please others. Is it in your voice?

Are you domesticating to what people say is cool and popular?

Try to dig deep and think about yourself as being wild and free.

How different is this person and her creativity to the person you are today?

Write a list.

Make it simple.

Unpack ways to discover where you may be domesticating yourself to fit the image of what others are projecting onto you.

Rest & Sleep

"Our creative selves need the space and time to think without noise, asking inspiration to arise. We need to have courage and give ourselves the space to truly think."

Doing Nothing

As the curtain raised I looked at the tissues in my hands from wiping the tears dripping down my face. I breathed and remembered the beauty of doing nothing.

I was sitting in a dark cinema after watching the film, Christopher Robin. It had me eating honey cake and wanting to use a linen napkin for the rest of my life.

This childhood tale filled with witty wisdom and heartfelt panoramas awakened the child within me. As each character tumbled out of the hundred-acre wood, I smiled and laughed out loud.

This movie follows the story of a grown-up, Christopher Robin and his struggle to make all the ends in his life meet. I sat there profoundly moved by the same conversations I recently had with my family.

How do we do it all?

Christopher walks into his house and smiles hesitantly at his wife;

"I'm sorry I got held up at work."

She looks at him with doubt, "You'll be working this weekend?"

He replies with shame "It can't be helped!"

The tension within a family to prioritise rest and fun, with work and the endless task list is one that we have not found an easy solution to. I sat listening to the conversations of this family trying to find their way through, smiling as Pooh came to be discovered by his old friend again.

The depth of imagination and the capacity it has to call you deeper into your internal dialogue was a timely reminder that sometimes doing nothing is everything.

> *Doing nothing often leads to the very best of something. Christopher Robin*

When was the last time you felt bored?

What about a weekend in the rambling countryside with no task list snuck in your briefcase?

DEAR CREATIVE SELF

As a culture, we are not great at doing nothing. Efficiency has us all held captive, and our mobile phones beep with constancy in our pockets. It means nothing for someone to message us late at night, and the myriad of connection points leave us all feeling a little disconnected.

> *Be completely humble and gentle; be patient, bearing with one another in love. Ephesians 4:2 (NIV)*

In some ways I believe it can be simply described as humility, to create spaces for patience. Work will always be there. We will never be able to completely finish every task list. However, our families will grow up. Our relationships can expire.

We need time that is free from task, pressure and stress. This film took me to space where I remembered what it was like to imagine as a child, roaming and wandering in nature. It had me making friends with my memories and reminding myself where my work belongs.

Pooh looks at Christopher Robin and innocently asks;

"Do you always carry that thing with you?"

Robin replies, "What my briefcase?"

And Pooh smiles innocently, "Yes, is it more important than a balloon?"

He curtly replies, "Of course it is more important than a balloon."

This little meet cute at the beginning of their newly formed relationship reminded me of how much more we place importance on our work and our sense of achievement and success, than fun and play.

I want to be known by my family and my loved ones by the attention I give to them. So they undoubtedly know that they are indeed my priority and although my heart dreams of far off places, that today I will sit in the discomfort of the present. I will make my priority known with my heart and my hands.

As creative people, it is imperative that we have times when we feel boredom. One of the most active environments for new ideas is doing nothing.

We need to remember to switch off and lay our briefcase of essential things down to rest. We can watch movies, throw popcorn and even buy a bunch of balloons.

We need to remember that sometimes doing nothing can lead to a great something. The letter in our creative lives that tells us we constantly need to be producing is not a healthy one.

More than ever, our world needs a reminder that taking a break and running away to the woods is never, ever a bad thing.

Dear Creative Self,

I am sorry for the times that I have packed our schedule so tight that I haven't given you space to breathe.

I know that productivity and social media likes are high fives to my people pleasing ways, but the best way to find the new is in a space of nothing.

When was the last time we had an afternoon of no plans, without should's, could's and have to's.

This weekend let's run away to the beach or a forest together and take no cameras or phones, telling no one.

Let's keep it a secret, just between us okay?

Yours truly,

Me

Creative Date

This one is pretty simple: book in time to do nothing. Set yourself a date in your calendar and write the word NOTHING in capitals.

Space

Rest

Reflection

Whether it is a whole day that we wipe aside and clear out for spontaneity, or it is a weekend away in a forest camping...

This space that we create is not a photo opportunity, it is just a space to allow boredom to grow and niggle at your soul.

Just like those little fish in Asia, that people allow to nibble away at their feet. Allow boredom to scour your soul sometime soon.

Clear space and do nothing.

Turn Off the Computer

Computers have bought great productivity to our creative ways but I am beginning to believe they are doing more damage than good. Especially in the creative arts and our expression. My dad is a creative, who has never made peace with his artisan soul.

He is a brilliant tinkerer. Always needing something in his hands to fix and play with, he is the ultimate fixer upper. His back shed is overflowing with tools and projects—he always has a project on the go.

This morning he beeped his horn out the front of our house and we laughed wondering what he was up to now. Sitting on our front driveway was a big Winnebago that he had just purchased.

The smile on his face as he walked towards our front door was hilarious. This truck—clearly full of tales of adventure—had seen many roads in its twenty years, and now had a new owner, with maps and stars in his eyes.

My Dad's generation was one of great dedication to the humble garden shed. Fixing bikes and lawnmowers, chatting over the back fence and reading manuals—Dad would often be found listening to the radio and musing over solutions.

All of these simple joys and pleasures have been lost in the depths of our computers. Instead of exploring the answers we are looking for from the depths of our own discovery, we search online and read forums of others' lessons learnt.

The art of creative expression is learning from the mistakes we have made and discovering a new way with our own hands. Some days we need to sink our hands into the tray of mismatched nails sitting on the musty garden shed bench to find the inspiration our soul requires.

Recently I went fishing with my family. As I was walking out the door in my sweat pants and old jumper, I ran back inside, took my phone out of my pocket and turned my computer off.

As I stood on the local jetty catching nothing, I breathed deep thinking about the answers my heart was searching for. The air in my lungs and a box of mismatched sinkers and hooks at my feet seemed to awaken my creative heart with feelings of deep satisfaction.

DEAR CREATIVE SELF

When was the last time you turned your computer off and found your solution at the bottom of a toolbox?

As a teenager I used to drive my family crazy tinkering around with sewing machines or clay or paint. The next minute I'd have my hands in a bowl making bread and then I would open a new pack of crayons. We were designed to have paint on our faces and flour wiped across our clothes. We have the capacity to dive deep into life and experience inspiration outside of a screen.

Life was designed in 4D, super sonic sound and when we immerse ourselves in the present, rather than someone else's creativity we grow. Turn off your computer this weekend and make something.

Go and hang in a garden shed and tinker. Smell the oil and the dust, pull out that canvas left unfinished and make something real.

Forget about what you are missing out online and fill up your cup with real life adventure. Close your laptop down and pack it away in its briefcase.

Real life.

Unfiltered.

TURN OFF THE COMPUTER

Dear Creative Self,

I know you want things to look pretty. But the creative process is brutal. You want all the stories to pile neatly on a page. You want the music to be soft and the light filtered. You want the pain in your shoulder and the chores in your house magically erased. We want pretty pictures in far off distant places to be the backdrop of your perfectly curated creative escapes. But creative self, innovation and pioneering are all about showing up to a blank page, with a half-cup of cold espresso and your imperfect life.

Creativity is trying something for the first time and documenting the story in the camera of our minds. Creativity is surrendering to a moment of inspiration that comes spontaneously at the most inconvenient moment.

Creativity is putting our work into places, and being often misunderstood where opinions roam free and large. The pursuit of the creative is to try and try again, allowing the thick skin that develops from delving deep within your soul to find space to breathe in the pursuit of beauty.

It's not pretty, or curated, or filtered but it's true deep beauty that calls deep to deep, light out of darkened places and glory shining through grey stormy places.

Show up again dear one.

Forget what the crowds are doing.

Stop trying to be someone else and shadow their pursuits.

What is happening deep within your today?

What lessons sing from yesterday?

And what hopes do you hold for tomorrow?

Yours truly,

Me

Creative Date

Today's creative date is to find something creative to do that is very messy. You could sign up for a colour run or ask your grandfather whether you can make something in his shed. You could pull out a piece of clay and get your hands covered in sticky residue. Dig up that half finished canvas and the paints laying at the bottom of your creativity shelf.

What does messy creativity do to your heart?

How does mess make you feel?

This is the pursuit of our creative selves, to begin something and in the midst of the mess continue until we find what needs to come next. Inspiration is often found in the very messy parts of our lives. These can be the moments of our greatest growth.

Embrace Silence

The sun was shining through the clouds and my foot kept shaking uncontrollably. Why had I signed up for this? The black wetsuit clung to every part of my body and the tank sitting on the harsh steel seat of the boat banged each and every time the waves formed across the horizon.

My then fiancé had convinced me to take a scuba diving course with him. He had been employed as a personal trainer to clients on a boat in the Caribbean and needed his scuba diving ticket. So every Saturday early in the morning we would turn up to the local pool learning everything we needed to know to gain the experience required to get our diving license.

The day had come to enter deep water off the coast of Rottnest, an island close to the Western Australian coastline. As I leaned back off the boat holding my equipment tightly I screamed, unsure of whether I would make it home that day.

The difference between the lessons in the safety of the Aquatic Centre and the open water, were all the unknown factors of nature in its full glory. Sharks, weather and waves all threatened the lessons I had learnt in the chlorine.

As I slowly made my way down to the bottom of the ocean, there was one thing that shocked me. It wasn't the fear of the unknown, it was the deadening silence that thrives deep in the ocean.

How do you go with silence?

Clarity comes knocking in its midst.

We live in a world of constant distractions, noise and shouting. Yet laying there beneath the waters of our shorelines, there is a whole world of silence, swimming back and forth. The ocean floor is a cacophony of color all swimming without noise.

Even thinking about that moment of complete surrender under water makes me want to slow down my breathing here sitting at my desk today. Breathing in deep the abandonment of our world and its constant mechanical whirrs.

When do you have the opportunity to sit in complete silence?

Our creative selves need the space and time to think without noise, asking inspiration to arise. We need to have courage and give ourselves the space to truly think.

Ideas are birthed when random collisions happen in our minds and then are captured by the possibility of our hands and hearts. Unless we have space between the birthing of an idea and the collection of its possibility, most ideas are crowded out and lost in the noise.

When we create space in our everyday schedules, to sit in silence, to breath deeply and truly listen to the thoughts, expressions and possibilities in our minds we give space to the birthing of new ideas.

Silence doesn't just happen in our world, we need to be active in finding moments and bringing in their beauty. It could be sitting in an old church downtown or when we wake up unexpectedly in the middle of the night, rather than trying desperately to fight our insomnia, settle into the silence and see what it has to say.

This is the potential of quiet moments of reflection.

These opportunities awaken just as the sun says hello to our day.

Capturing moments of complete surrender and facing our fears that try to scare us away from the peace.

Embrace the silence and surrender to the unknown.

EMBRACE SILENCE

Dear Creative Self,

There are moments of peace and silence that are waiting. You often try to escape them in busyness and this one hurried life. What if you surrendered to silence? I know fear is found in those moments of quiet. The beauty of your one life of challenge, courage and brilliance can be unlocked here.

Silence makes the future look bleak. It also reminds you how truly alone you are. This stark reality is but a moment until you reconcile the past and step into the future.

Noise makes you forget your deep reoccurring reminders that you were not created for this world. There are sacred sounds found in the space of receiving.

What if you opened yourself to filling up again, rather than always giving out?

Breathe in the good things found in silence.

Breathe out the heartache and pain.

Reawaken the possibility of a new day.

Clarity is waiting there.

This is where the deep calls unto deep.

Yours truly,

Me

Creative Date

Today's creative date is to set aside time and surrender to silence. It might be a walk along the ocean, with no podcast or music in your ears. It could be a time sitting in the middle of a local bushland, surrendered to a moment of quiet. You could go and sit in an old church, on a wooden pew and think.

Here's how you could plan it;

1. Book a time in your diary that is not negotiable, with the worries and pressures of life.
2. I want you to set aside 30 minutes.
3. Leave your phone at home.
4. When you get home, just write one word that came to you in the midst of the silence.

Embrace the silence, dear creative self, deep rest is waiting.

Go To Sleep

The clock ticked over, as I lay awake, begging my brain to slow down. "Amanda, sleeeeeep, you need to sleep."

The more I begged my eyes to stay closed, the more awake my heart and brain became. There was a loud snore coming from the comatose male next to me and it nearly broke me.

I need to sleep.

Please help me sleep.

No more ideas.

And breathe.

It had been a season of broken sleep with a newborn and a toddler. My restless sleep made everything cloudy. Each cry that awoke my weary soul in the middle of the night was like a scraping of nails down a chalkboard. As I lay there in bed, after eventually getting one of my children asleep, the next would wake and my heart felt like it was ready to stop beating.

I was desperate for a night of unbroken sleep and even when I got a night to myself, I couldn't sleep because of the debt and habits that had collated.

Have you ever suffered insomnia at the hands of someone else?

Maybe that work deadline was looming and procrastination held you captive. Those seasons where sleep eludes you as you ponder a conversation over and over in your mind until you find the right words. The creative dreamer can roll over and over in bed, as they fight for clarity in the waking hours of the moment with both dark and light.

The rhythm of a creative soul can be at the mercy of inspiration, procrastination and deadlines. As we lie in bed each night it can be the perfect time of awakening when a new idea sparks.

Over the last year as I have regained a regular sleeping pattern it has helped every area of my life to thrive. Especially in showing up to my creative self. I have implemented simple disciplines that I need to tell my creative self, to let go and surrender to sleep. These simple small changes have completely changed the way I prioritise sleep for my creative self.

I have a 10pm screen curfew, no matter the deadline I am facing. I bought a cheap alarm clock for my bedside and started charging my phone in another room, so I am not tempted to scroll Social Media in the middle of the night. I put an essential oil diffuser next to my bedside table, so each night I'm breathing in lavender oil as I am falling asleep. I read a paperback book just for a few chapters to let my mind start to slow down. I limit my coffee intake to two cups a day and I have a sleep meditation that I play over and over, if I find myself awake early in the morning before the sun has risen.

There are many studies that tell creatives as a collective that the regular art of sleeping well, will help your creativity thrive. Sleep clears the cobwebs and helps you think clearer, which means less mistakes. Routine can often be the last thing that you want, but your body will thank you.

> *When you lie down, you will not be afraid; when you lie down, your sleep will be sweet. Proverb 3: 24 (NIV)*

You will write better, think more clearly and find ways to reinvent what has always been accepted as normal. Pioneering new ideas as a creative soul takes energy, and your mind needs time to recalibrate.

What are some simple changes you could make in your sleeping routine today?

Our creative minds desperately need a simple rhythm of sleep—if you travel often for your work, the need for this can be even more magnified.

The greater your sleep rhythm is collated, the more it creates opportunities for your body to recalibrate and hear the stories that might be holding you captive. Find a friend to hold you accountable to your late night Social Media binges. No matter what you do, find ways to get a regular seven hours of deep, restorative sleep.

It truly will change your productivity, mental health and creativity.

GO TO SLEEP

Dear Creative Self,

Let's talk about sleep. Your mind races with worries and new ideas. You leave deadlines right to the last minute and then you burn your energy in trying to meet the expectations of others.

I know sleep eludes you sometimes. I know that worries about things you cannot change hold you captive. What if you made some simple routines that helped you recover and dream again?

Sleep, begets sleep.

Rest brings us to a place of health and wellbeing.

You desperately want to bring change to this area of your daily wrestle. You must make a commitment to change. As you lean into new opportunities, creative pursuits and potential what if the key that was missing to unlock the next part of your journey was just sleep!

Seek out the space between where you used to be and the longing for tomorrow. New spaces of belief can be developed within the cocoon of our bedroom.

Sleep, dear one, find rest.

Breathe in deep the possibilities of another tomorrow.

Pushing through only works for a short time.

Breathe out the worries of this world.

Yours truly,

Me

Creative Date

Today's creative date is to choose one of the tools I have created to help bring some micro changes to your sleep routine.
- Choose a time to turn off screens.
- Charge your phone in another room from where you sleep.
- Buy a cheap alarm clock for your bedside table.
- Diffuse lavender oil or sprinkle it on your pillow.
- Read a couple of chapters of a paperback book as you go to sleep.
- Stop drinking caffeine or too many drinks after 5pm.
- Drink a cup of chamomile tea as you are going into your sleep routine.
- Have a hot shower and put a hot water bottle in your bed for comfort.
- Set a regular time each day to go to sleep and wake up.

Write out your sleep schedule and ask a friend to hold you accountable, especially to late night television and Social Media bingeing.

Technology

"Change is a constant in our world and no matter what happens there will always be new ways of doing things. Digging our heels in to say I will not move only holds us captive to the pain of progress in the long run."

Digital Detox

Four billion people have access to the Internet and more than half of them have smart phones. Three billion people access Social Media platforms every single day. At a scroll of a finger we can communicate globally but many of us struggle to find the words to say hello to our neighbour. We are more isolated than even before and health professionals in Australia have recently found that the impact of isolation on our health is just as life threatening today as smoking fifteen cigarettes.

Social Media has broken all the rules and blurred the lines between knowledge and presence. The human condition is birthed in the presupposition that we belong. Village life, communities and family units were the foundation stones of our existence, yet we have seen them morph into relationships of convenience rather than belonging.

Every day I am surrounded by hundreds of people—I have thousands of friends and followers online yet I feel more disconnected and alone than ever before. To be busy is seen as successful, and all the promises that technology gave us about productivity and connection are beginning to show us a false negative reading. Finding friendship in a disconnected world is a challenge, especially when technology is the indicator of our identity and belonging.

We are distracted, always with a quick scroll as we sit waiting to quell our boredom. We are disconnected because we believe we know everything about the people around us as they have over shared online.

The filters, the promises of overnight success and the fake news disillusion us. We sit in cafes scrolling whilst our loved ones sit across from us, all of us unsure how to bridge the gap of disconnect.

Over the last few years, I have taken one day a week off social media and for one month every year I log off. However, I am realising that rather than keeping to these boundaries that are used as emergency measures, I needed to reframe the role of technology in my creativity and life.

One of the first ways that you can work on mastering technology, is truly thinking about what you are posting about and why. Each time someone likes or comments on our posts there is a hit of dopamine that makes us feel good in the immediate but depletes us when we are constantly bombarded.

When we become accustomed to this feeling it can soon turn into a habit that means we are posting for the sake of posting without truly having something meaningful to say.

1. Turn off all the notifications on all your social media sites. Every time a notification comes on it distracts you and compounds this addiction.
2. Set aside a time each day that you will post. No more than one post time per day.
3. Prepare what you are going to post before you open the site. Sit with a brainstorming page, write out your caption in a different mechanism and think mindfully before you post.
4. Be aware when you are rushing through the social media site, or mindlessly scrolling. Press pause answering these questions.

* Am I hiding from something?
* Am I just bored?
* Is there a more connected way I can use this time?
* What can I produce to bring satisfaction in this window of time?

Lastly, train yourself to sit with the post in front of you, rather than swiping past, let yourself engage.

Dear Creative Self,

I know the instant gratification of those online spaces is addictive and makes you feel like you belong. There is something better, though, that calls us into a new season of grace. It is looking into the eyes of someone sitting across the table from you. It is having a private conversation, without worrying about who might come across your thoughts. It is changing your mind, mid sentence as you listen carefully to the body language of the person with you, and realise maybe you were wrong.

Honour the people in your presence, more than those who slide into Direct Message's online. Chat about ideas, think boldly out loud and wonder what makes friendship real.

Breathe in the atmosphere of a room, rather than the square image from someone online.

Let's give space and time to think again.

Are you ready for change?

Tomorrow will be better.

Yours truly,

Me

Creative Date

Today's creative date is to take a seven-day break from social media.

Don't do a big announcement; just take seven days to recalibrate.

Your creative self will thank you, for the space and the opportunity to recover. You may need to delete apps off your phone. You might need to tell a friend for accountability.

The space to recreate again, for no one but the sheer beauty of discovering creativity, waits.

Unoffendable

I was sitting on the second row in a university theatre watching a live stream of a speaker encouraging us to live a generous life. There in the midst of that beautiful atmosphere, he said a quick throw away sentence, that reverberated around the room.

He said this: "my wife and I just made a decision a long time ago that we were the unoffendables"

Unoffendable. What a great non-word!

How are you going in the area of offence?

I have realised across my life, there are many opportunities every week to live offended. It arises in my parenting. My little people say things that sink deeper into my heart that I realise. I have decided that I will be unoffendable in my parenting.

In our online spaces, where opinions run rife, post after post, I have realised that we have every opportunity to be offended, multiple times a day. I have made the decision not to allow offence to mark my online space.

Offence comes every day in my relationships. Little off hand comments that were not intentioned, but really do sting, maybe our ego. Being left out of invitations, people using us in ways that we weren't expecting—despite these moments of heart I have made a decision to be unoffended in my relationships.

You see, this doesn't mean we don't have boundaries; it just means we don't allow offence and bitterness to creep into our hearts. It is an issue of our hearts, not what happens to us but the ways that we respond to those moments.

Offence is one of the main emotions that will keep you small. Bitterness sits in a place within our soul and rots away our perception of people, places and memories. Offence is the way we carry around in our backpacks the hurts that have come to haunt and steal the joy we own.

Offence is a choice. I promise you can learn to not let fear and offence to take hold of your heart and your reactions, by setting boundaries when we don't allow others' behaviour to impact our internal places of peace and restoration.

We have every reason to live offended. In fact the Internet has created a whole industry out of it. Offence is something that will happen every day if we allow it. But I truly believe that offence can be shaken off.

Find ways to let go, to surrender, to forgive, to reinvent, to heal, to unpack and recalibrate.

Does that mean we ignore the emotions that come when dealing with people?

Of course it doesn't, but offence is when we allow something small to niggle its way into our hearts and the only person it holds captive is ourselves.

This is why I love my community that we gather with every Sunday and through the week, because it's a group of imperfect people growing in capacity and learning to begin again.

If offence has found its way into your heart, I totally get it, but it is the one thing that is going to keep you contained.

The minute we release those places of offence, a lightness and freedom comes. The capacity to dream again arrives on our doorstep and trust bubbles to the surface again.

What if we as a generation became known as the unoffendables?

Rather than the offended!

You can do more in a position of hope than cynical reclined opinions. Be a lover not a hater. There is power in encouragement. There is power in returning a difficult situation with love and forgiveness.

Offence renders us useless.

It's not that we can't be angry at injustice. Anger is a powerful tool that can propel us, if we find ways to harness its power and use it for the benefit of the greater good.

Are there places of offence in your heart?

When you see a particular person, does your skin bristle?

This is an opportunity to release offence, to allow forgiveness to come and replace those pieces in our history and surrender us into new opportunities.

Offence will always weigh you down heavily. Like a backpack full of rocks, shadows and difficult memories, that weighs down your every day walking places.

Lay that backpack down, unpack the offences that have piled up. It doesn't take much to find the stories we are carrying around in our everyday lives.

Leave them behind at an altar of grace, purpose and wide-open spaces of love. Dance like the weight has been lifted and release yourself from the running narratives that hold you in those patterns.

The unoffendables.

Dear Creative Self,

Breathe in forgiveness and let go of those stories you have been telling yourself. Freedom is waiting at the other side of laying down your cynicism.

Those offence dialogues have often kept you locked down in a pattern of regret and pain. It's time to let go of those people that play around inside your memories. Don't keep replaying over and over those feelings, sentences and weights that kept you contained.

You want to begin again.

Forget those negative places that held your heart tight and unsure.

Choose to let go.

Whether what happened was okay or not. Whether it was a big story or something that just added up, week after week. Those moments that you wanted to shout from the top of my lungs, "You cannot keep doing this to me!"

Forgiveness does not mean forgetting, it just creates beautiful boundaries around what you allow to define your identity.

Believe the best and decide what truly you want to give your energy to.

You will lay down that backpack of offence and not allow it to define you.

Yours truly,

Me

Creative Date

Today's creative date is to sit in a café and write a letter to your offences. Write a letter to those memories that have held you captive. Or write a poem to those people who will never read your words to release them from your offence.

It can be angry or devastating. Allow perspective to rise from the ashes of offence.

You can burn your letters, or throw them away in a rubbish bin. You can find a friend to send your precious words to, or allow them to sit in your journal.

Find a way to release and let go of those places that hold you captive.

Release, let go and begin again.

We all hold offence, just some of us have learnt ways to let go and begin again.

Chase Dreams over Platforms

I often get asked to speak on the topic of Social Media and can I tell you a secret? It makes me mad. Like angry, served with a side of "What am I even doing with my life?"

The reason I am frustrated is that I don't want to perpetuate what is already a toxic part of our worlds. I don't want to add my opinion to the rushing tide of noise.

My relationship with the online world is like a needy best friend. I pretty much vow most weeks I am going to cancel all my social media accounts and do something more productive with my life. Then I find a story like this email that landed today in my inbox that ended with...

"Anyway I just wanted to thank you for your words, I needed them that day!" Another came the day after, "My plan for this year is to set aside more intentional time to write so thanks for prompting me and sparking excitement in me. Be encouraged; you are helping me and so many others to tell our stories."

I breathe in deeply and I remember the power of story. Your story, my story, and our story together.

I remember the importance of our shared conversations and I remind myself to find a way to wade through the mud and discover a mid-point again with my addiction to screens. My addiction to people's approval of my ideas and life, and my addiction to doing something (procrastinating) instead of showing up to my dreams

Are you addicted to scrolling?

We need together to encourage one another to chase dreams not platforms. Our society tells our creative selves that the way to feel strong and successful is to build bigger platforms. There is nothing wrong with influential places

I am allowing myself to dream again in a way that is bold and courageous, allowing opportunity finding me waiting, rather than bashing down the doors of platforms that seem enticing but are just chasing the wind.

We live in an age of platform building. Grandstanding, shouting our agendas from behind our keyboards and then feeling frustrated when the connection feels less than real.

We live in an age where we believe that a waterfall of money is awaiting the click funnel we have found ourselves down, and just one more thing will be the releasing of our worldwide success.

We live in an age of self-made ambition, and in essence, there is sheer beauty in seeing the underdog rise up and find His voice but at the expense of what?

My family or physical health, mental load and stress?

No thanks.

When we focus on the platforms we are building, as a badge of honour for worth and worthiness, then we begin to tumble and fall.

When we allow the dreams in our hearts, to bubble like my sourdough starter sitting on my bench, something happens in the process. It is the beginning of the process of change.

We were created to produce my friends, not consume. If we feed the monkey that is the belief that we deserve the rights to have platforms that we stand and shout our messages from, the beast grows.

What if we chased dreams over platforms?

The platforms may come to you, my friend, the opportunity for influence may rise and find us waiting, but this is a by-product of living a life of alignment.

Dear Creative Self,

I am sorry for the times that I have shamed myself in the midst of my creative process. When I have said that a creative pursuit was worthless because it didn't get the recognition I was expecting with likes, shares and follows online.

I'm sorry for the times I have gone down rabbit holes looking for a quick fix to bring thousands of accolades.

Can you begin again? Pick up that blank piece of paper. Write for you and not the crowd. Show up and own your brave stories that changed your life not your bank account. If platforms come and go, promise to be the same person in the green rooms as you are on the stage.

Forget those quick fixes of buying people's affections by saying what you think they want you to say, rather than the truth.

I am sorry that I think something is more important when people acknowledge it, rather than just the sheer beauty of being true for us in that moment.

Let's begin again shall we?

Yours truly,

Me

Creative Date

Today's creative date is to find a big piece of paper. In the centre of the paper I want you to draw a circle.

Inside the circle I want you to write the names of the people who really matter to you. Who holds you accountable? The names of those people who will give you honest feedback but at the same time encouragement so that your dreams come alive.

These people are those whose opinion matters.

Now outside of that circle write the names of those people that you often try to please with your creativity. Write the names of those people who criticize you or try to give you their opinion and it makes you feel small.

These people are those whose opinions need to run off you like water.

This exercise is a powerful tool to help you recalibrate whether you are chasing platforms or dreams. Whether you are chasing people's opinions or the very core of your values and vision.

Nothing New Under the Sun

Our world is constantly changing. Every weekend a new business is launched and the news tells us a new formula for success. We live in a constant cycle of change. Some days I get decision fatigue from all the options that are given to me in our modern world.

Emails fling at us and notifications pile up. A new social media stream launches and pockets of the world go looking for their new online high. In the midst of all this change and challenge, I have decided one thing as a creative finding ways to learn and grow: I will be an early adopter of change.

Change is a constant in our world and no matter what happens there will always be new ways of doing things. Digging our heels in to say I will not move only holds us captive to the pain of progress in the long run.

I find it difficult sometimes to transition change. There is a stubbornness that arises in my stance. I am learning that flexibility is a powerful trait as a creative to be open for new ideas and ways.

As we surrender to the opportunity of doing something different, we find new ways to do things we never thought we could.

When you hear about a new website, app or event what is your first response?

Do you roll your eyes in exasperation or do you surrender to the potential of learning something new?

The creative pursuit is the opportunity to find new ways of doing things that you have never done before. When we are open to seeing new things, asking questions and sitting in the seat of the learner, flexibility comes swiftly.

Lately I have been learning that it is as simple as leaning in, rather than leaning back in cynicism. It's as easy as downloading that new app and exploring, ready to learn and grow.

Being an early adopter as a creative means that we face the cynicism that we have tried it all before. We also need to challenge the notion that everything under the sun has been created before and we are just in wash cycle of beginning it again.

I absolutely believe that this is not true. For example there was never a smart phone before a team of creative people designed it. What about Netflix? It was just an idea in someone's mind, before it became the new cultural phenomena that it has become today. Also, Facebook was something that had never been seen before it was coded in a university bedroom.

There are songs that have never been written before and ideas that will change the productivity of our world. When we sit in the seat of cynic and tell ourselves that we have nothing new to learn, we will shrink back from the possibility found in the midst of trying something new.

The writer Solomon said in the book of Ecclesiastes that there is nothing new under the sun. However he was in a place of lament and sheer brokenness. He was complaining about the monotony of our everyday life. We can easily become like Solomon when we get our sustenance from things rather than an everlasting source of creativity, possibility and brilliance.

There is always new coming. New mercies in the morning, new opportunities, and great ideas colliding in the middle of the skies.

As a creative soul, lean in when something new is on the horizon. Be the first of your friends to download it and explore its hidden spaces. Talk with your friends about ideas rather than people. Encourage one another to step out into the dreams, desires and possibilities hidden in our hearts.

Not only did Solomon write about the monotony of life and how nothing gives him pleasure any more, he also wrote proverbs of wisdom to remind himself of what success truly is measured by.

> Their purpose is to teach people to live disciplined and successful lives, to help then do what is just, right and fair. Proverbs 1:3 (NIV)

I am learning that when I lean into the wisdom of those from days gone by, but reach into the liminal space of the unknown, I am drawn into new days of possibility.

We can let go of cynicism and find the possibility of trying something new, and I believe that is where the grace lies. There is sheer terror in jumping off the ledge, as we are often afraid of the greatness in our hearts and lives rather than falling.

I do believe there are many new things under the sun. Together find ways to explore what is coming on the horizon. Watch new businesses start to explode and ideas percolate.

Be someone who cheers on the pioneers, those who are trying to do something that hasn't been done before. It is a crazy, scary place to live but the rewards of actualizing the dreams in your heart are profound.

Dear Creative Self,

Let's not run away from the fear of trying something for the first time. I know that you have been burnt. People have told you that they have seen it all before, done it all and bought the t-shirt.

There are sprinkles of dew in the early morning light that reflect the moment of possibility that a new day is dawning.

Look at the dew. Remember the fresh presence of God and his calling of you into open and wide places.

There is a new light shining its spotlight upon the potential of tomorrow.

I know you have held ideas in your heart that others have taken. I know that the moment you allow yourself to try to believe again, then a notification pops up that someone else has discovered your idea too.

No matter, just continue to press on. With new ideas, open hands and hearts. When you surrender to the great adventure of it all, brilliance is there waiting.

Thanks for the moments of surrender.

Yours truly,

Me

DEAR CREATIVE SELF

Creative Date

Today's creative idea is to take a piece of paper and write a list of all the ideas that have been bubbling in your mind for years.

Those crazy teenage adventures you planned in journals—those late night, after-too-much-pizza-book-ideas. Ideas from those moments when we believed we could do anything and dreamed again.

Write a list of what you could do!

Not what you should do.

But what could you do in the future.

And be bold enough to go and share the ideas with a safe creative friend.

Innovation

"If you look across history, human wisdom and tenacity has been recorded through story. I strongly believe that somebody needs your story. The highs, the lows, the in-betweens and the not enough yet."

Ruminate

The definition of rumination is to chew the cud. The most skilled creative technicians are those who allow ideas to ruminate, process and brew.

We live in a society that is continually asking us to hurry up. We're a consumer-focused community that frequently asks for more and then quickly throws away our ideas and produce like the trash.

The appetite of our social media beast means that creatively, our ideas can be thrown away for another fad that is coming up on the horizon.

Do you have an idea that you have been ruminating on for a decade?

There is nothing wrong with the waiting process for idea development. Each term I run a writers retreat with a small group of women. Recently we went to a Spanish monastery, hidden in the Australian outback.

As I sat in the library of this ancient building, there was a moment of deep satisfaction as I allowed myself to celebrate the fact that I had been thinking about this very moment for about fifteen years.

The little moments in-between, when I would dream of a writers gathering, where writers would spend time walking among the vineyards, gathered to find their collective imagination again.

I spent fifteen years ruminating on this dream—a decade and a half of idea collection.

Then one day, I decided it was time to bring this little dream to life. So I put pen to paper, then my fingers rested upon the keyboard. I created a post, an event page and sent the invites out. Then people responded, we set the date and booked the venue.

A little bit of time passed and then we packed some clothes, I gathered some gifts, and we drove miles upon miles to show up.

This is the art of ruminating.

Philippians 4: 8: says it this way:

Finally, brothers and sisters, whatever is true, whatever is noble, whatever is right, whatever is pure, whatever is lovely, whatever is admirable, if anything is excellent or praiseworthy, think about such things.

We need times of thinking and then seasons of sowing. Then the time comes to lean into the idea and to have a go.

What seeds are you sowing in your thought life today that can be harvested tomorrow?

We are often stuck in one of these phases.

We skip the waiting.

We keep ruminating and don't move into courage.

Or we forget the very idea and seed that was planted long ago.

The greatest gift in the art of rumination is creating time to think. We live in a world that fills the spaces in between with a lot of noise. I have found that ruminating happens in the margins.

Rumination happens as we fall asleep. It is the moments when we are listening to worship and surrendering to the possibility of 'could'. It takes place in a hot shower where we chew the cud, process the potential and allow our imaginations to run wild and free.

Do you feel stuck?

We need to allow ourselves to be bored enough to think about possibilities. We also need to have the courage to not shut down an idea if we are not in the season to see it come to pass. It is all about hope and courage.

To take the moments to begin again and think that it could be just in the waiting. It is not about letting go of the idea; it is just to chew it over again and again.

Dream again daydreamer, maybe the idea that has been hidden in the back of your mind, is ready to be birthed. This letter is awaiting reformation.

Dear Creative Self,

Thank you for the ideas that have been birthed in the midst of pain. I know that sometimes you get stuck. I know that often you feel frustrated by the process of creating. Allow the confusion you feel to teach you a path through. It is a signpost that there is a new way.

Today though I want you to know that the idea you have carried for decades is not a weight. Sometimes it feels like a backpack you're carrying, where each idea is like a rock. Today I want you to know that the time you have given thinking and dreaming is not wasted.

Together let's continue to believe for new ideas but also have the courage to birth the ideas that we have carried for decades.

The season has shifted and waned, but maybe just maybe it is time to put pen to paper.

Thanks for believing in my potential; even when I had forgotten about the seeds I carried inside.

Yours truly,

Me

Creative Date

Today's task is to take out a big piece of paper and dump everything out of your mind.

Grab four coloured pens, assigning these four categories to each colour.

Now

Next

Delegate

Dream

Often we get stuck in the birthing of creative ideas because we need a scaffold around the how, rather than the what.

When we divide our tasks into these simple categories it brings great clarity.

Rather than the overwhelming feeling of how can I do this? we start to come back to the simple four quadrants that help you to find a way through the mess.

Collect Memories

There is a craft to being creative. I am often misunderstood at dinner parties and categorised as unusual.

When someone asks me what I do, I dance around with, "I'm a writer, in the spiritual or self-help kind of categories."

Then comes the slow head tilt. If only they knew how difficult it is to actually capture the beauty of a moment. Maybe they wouldn't be so quick to swipe left on our interaction.

There may not be a science degree that validates the pain of the creative process, but there are many ways that the craft of creativity is a skilled art form.

I believe everyone is creative but it takes intentionality to grow this muscle in our lives.

Every part of our being is founded in the breath of inspiration. There is something only you can bring to this earth. It's as unique as your thumbprint, your DNA—it is your essence.

I belong to a Christian tradition and there is a story of creation that we can draw inspiration from.

I believe we are made in the image of a creative God, and we reflect His creativity. When we speak to our creative selves, we are reigniting a conversation that has been happening since the beginning of time.

He spoke and the world came to life. A spoken word birthed a river. A sky that flashed with pink developed from the breath He breathed into it. Then He spoke breath into the ground and humanity arose.

There is a scaffold to creating, and I believe it comes back to the beginning in the same way that we were designed to give intentional time to find creativity. Across our week, we can bring shape and space to give our creative selves time to document and store up memories for the future. I have been studying an Australian bird called the bowerbird.

This species is the ultimate hoarder of the animal kingdom. These birds are collectors and build architectural masterpieces with their nests. They roam the forest looking for little objects and treasures on the ground, to make a home to nest in.

The burrow that they create can be filled with ropes and ties, sticks, rocks and leaves. The little creative space this bird makes is profoundly architectural in the middle of the Australian bush.

How do you think about your creative process and collect your memories?

I would begin thinking about the scaffold of your week.

You could start by dedicating a day and time for your creative pursuits and writing down the memories, the feelings, sounds and emotions that are unveiled amid the moments of your week.

We can be a collector of moments, things, images, quotes, inspirations, stories and beautiful memories. If we don't create a system to process through, and document these ordinary everyday moments, they just fly past us and are forgotten.

What scaffold do you use to collect and categorise your creative musings?

We have a creative self that is collecting emotions and memories from every moment that we enter. When we walk into a room, we smell the atmosphere, we feel impressions from those who are around us, we hear sounds.

Unless we take the time to document and give these ideas space to grow, they will be lost in the moment.

When we breathe life into our memories and create a scaffold that carries them into our tomorrow, we have something to begin our creative process with.

> Make a careful exploration of who you are and the work you have been given, and then sink yourself into that. Don't be impressed with yourself. Don't compare yourself with others. Each of you must take responsibility for doing the creative best you can with your own life. Galatians 6:4-5 (NIV)

There is a space for you to wrestle with your identity and sink yourselves into that. Rather than being impressed with ourselves, what if we found ways to collect the beauty around us. Taking responsibility to do our creative best. Collecting the inspiration in your everyday rather than allowing it just to slip through your fingers.

It can be as simple as a notebook that only holds creative ideas, memories and moments that are not tasks or things to do. You could create a note file on your phone where you write a word or store an image that becomes a reminder.

Just as a bowerbird collects little memories to create an environment and home, so can we.

These memories we collect become the starting point of our ideas in the future. If you learn the art of pilgrimage, finding a way to store these memories, your moments of inspiration will be collated in a form that creates a scaffold for the new in your life.

COLLECT MEMORIES

Dear Creative Self,

We have always been together, through the highs and lows and in-betweens. Together in those days that we would rather forget, moments when fear overcame us and we were unsure whether we would ever make it through.

Then there were those miracle moments. The mountain top adventures, when we breathed in the taste of victory and actually making it through.

I remember those moments when we carried the emotions that were unveiled deep within our soul, unsure we would ever recover from the train wreck.

Thank you for collecting my emotions like jewels.

Thank you for reaching into my pockets and collecting my tears with a pretty blue jar.

Thankyou for coming alongside me, in those moments that I wished I could escape from.

Every memory that we have created together has formed and shaped the person that you are today. Strong and then unsure. Soft yet capable.

Each memory unravels the beauty of the present for my future inspiration. I promise I won't shame you for actually feeling.

I want to take the time to sit in the truth of the awakening you are referencing. Rather than squashing down my feelings, being curious with what lessons they are teaching me.

Thank you for always being there.

Yours truly,

Me

Creative Date

Today's creative date is all about walking through nature, like a curious bowerbird to collect memories. Take a jar and walk along the ocean. Pick up shells, and sticks, smoothed glass and little flowers. Look for little memories that will inspire you in the future.

When you get home, what if you pull out a blank piece of paper and use one of these little memories you collected to write a story. Sit and free-write about the texture, the shade of the sun and how it makes you feel.

What about writing from a different perspective, character or tone?

You could paint a picture with words or write a poem. A simple reminder of the moment— to document the inconsequential simplicities that are often lost in the busyness of our day.

The Boredom Basket

Arriving early to the school gate is my daily reality. Once I have finished an appointment or done the grocery shopping, rather than drive home, I slide into the car park and I'm one of the first parents there, in the heat of my car. It is then that the boredom of my daily reality creeps in.

These moments, as I wait in the car or I am sitting in a café, not wanting to show up to my blank page, are the places that I often scroll rather than surrender.

How do you handle boredom?

The habits of our in-between moments can make or break the creative process. We want to paint, but don't want to face the canvas so we enter into the procrastination place. We know that there is a story waiting to be captured but the pain of piecing together the words below the surface irritates us towards the boredom dance.

Do you find creativity illusive sometimes?

The pain of showing up to serve the creative ideas gifted to us by God, asks discipline of us that sometimes is just too hard to acknowledge. That is why we scroll. This is where addictions come into our creative spaces and draw our attention away from the pain of growth.

Recently I decided to make a basket full of things that I could grab instead of my phone. Often procrastination involves scrolling and consuming here online. However when we produce, it creates a catalyst for us to bring our best to our writing/creative/purpose driven space.

The easiest way to copy others is to fill your life with the thoughts and moments of them, rather than finding your own ideas, revelations and inspirations from the times you gives yourself permission to have space.

Space to produce for no one except you. Space to process the emotions that have been squashed down. Space to breathe.

This creates time to pray and meditate on the good. Helping us understand what is worthy, holy and sacred for ourselves. These moments of boredom become like a boiling kettle, heating up the ideas inside of you.

DEAR CREATIVE SELF

If we continue to consume rather than produce and engage online we will increasingly feel frustrated from grazing off the fields of others rather than planting seeds in our own field.

What would be in your boredom basket?

Lately I have been leaving a library book in my car so I can use my time more wisely as I wait for my kids to finish school. I also use these times to record some live videos for my readers, so I can recreate the habits that hold me captive.

Next time you go to grab your phone, or computer or Netflix remote, what if you grabbed your boredom basket and began to write, make or create to heal. Let's get bored together and make something that brings life and inspiration.

Dear Creative Self,

You are wired for stimulation. You wrestle sometimes to bring forth the insight and wisdom that has been so generously given. New ideas often need new soil and surrender of those moments in-between.

I give you permission to dream, explore, imagine and dance with delight. Rather than absorbing the ideas of others, what if you created a new routine for boredom that brings forth great inspiration.

You can do great things. There is a new solution in waiting, there is a manuscript that has been hiding. A song is blossoming and a series of paintings has been waiting to birth. A television script is brewing and a movie full of creative insight wants to reveal its face.

Time brings inspiration and new wine. Moments of deep recalibration of what can be possible between God and us.

You are a vessel of delight and pure beauty, when you surrender those moments everyday and look for the brilliance found in the wrestle.

Pick up something to wrestle with. Find some clay that is waiting to form a new idea and inspiration. Reframe those bored moments into spaces of producing rather than consuming.

Explore and breathe life into those moments in-between allowing boredom to birth the new.

Yours truly,

Me

Creative Date

Today's creative date is to find a basket. Drop into that basket all the unfinished projects you have not wanted to face. It could be a journal or a book. It could be a crochet project or a knitted scarf waiting for completion. Maybe you could add in a crossword puzzle or a little box full of clay.

There is a process to creativity that involves procrastination. It is easy to become a consumer of other people's creativity rather than a producer of your own creative ideas.

The greatest times of idea calibration are in those boredom moments. Today's goal is to create a box of things that are non-technology based to get bored with.

What are the projects in your cupboard that are unfinished?

You could throw them in the basket and finish them.

Ask Great Questions

I stood in the classroom waiting for the smack down as a Mother asked to speak with me. My internal defence mechanisms shot up and I said, "Here we go," silently. Yesterday, your daughter asked me a question.

I said "Yes and?" watching this heavily pregnant Mum tentatively move from foot to foot.

She said "Excuse me, is it possible that I could come on an excursion to see you give birth to your baby?" We both looked at each other and burst out laughing.

My daughter is a leader. She is creative, bold and tenacious, but these are not the things, that make her a leader. I know she is a leader because she constantly asks great questions.

In school this gets kids into trouble; we are taught to stop asking questions and to toe the line. There are boundaries that create boxes around students to help teachers keep twenty-six children quiet.

Asking great questions reframes our capacity to change culture and do things differently. Every person who has changed the history of our world has asked a question they didn't know the answer to.

When there was no telephone, someone asked a question that had no answer. When there was no computer, someone asked a question about storing thoughts somewhere other than our brains. When there was no food delivery service, someone asked the question why not?

Questioning the 'what is', to bring about something new can be the most powerful tool for transformation. As we answer questions about our own lives, we grow in self-awareness.

We can carry a fear of questions that comes from the pressure of taking tests and exams at school—but as we learn to dig deep into our creative selves we find the answers that are right for our own stories and the power to pioneer something new.

What questions are you avoiding out of fear?

Recognising this can be such an amazing process of personal growth and overcoming, to find ways to answer the questions that we are hiding from.

As a creative, it can be difficult to find surety in a world that is always changing. Often creative souls can struggle with questions because we are constantly trying to make sense out of suffering. Each and every time we wrestle with things that we do not have answers for, as we start to unravel the knots of complexity, we find our voice more and more.

There is nothing wrong with not having all the answers—actually as a creative soul if you have answers for everything you stop seeking. It is in the wrestle; it is in the seeking place that we make new discoveries and find ways that have never been done before.

What if there is another way?

How come we have always done it like this?

We could do something like this, couldn't we?

Questions are provokers to find a different way. Our creative selves were designed to discover the new. Without a question being asked, we just keep doing what we have always done.

ASK GREAT QUESTIONS

Dear Creative Self,

Keep asking the questions that no one wants to answer. Keep on thinking about that problem you cannot escape from. Yes there is another way; in fact, there are thousands of answers to the question you ponder.

When you just accept the culture of our day as being correct and the way it has always been, you start to flow into a lake of stagnancy.

Wrestle with questions.

What if you became known for the leadership gift on your life, because of the questions that you ask to delve deeper into the moments presented to you?

It takes courage to be a question asker.

Fear sneaks up behind you and whispers, stop getting in the way all the time; just do what everyone else is doing. Questions are the training ground of the world's greatest leaders and you are leaning into the new because of the reflecting and thinking you are doing.

Don't despise the whys that comes up in your mind. Find ways to celebrate them and explore the possibility of the not yet.

Let's ask another question.

Yours truly,

Me

Creative Date

Today's creative date is all about answering questions for self-awareness. Sit with a journal, this book and these questions and start to write. Take the time to journal for yourself, not for anyone else. Self-awareness can be a scary prospect. The more we understand ourselves the greater our growth and potential. Each time I sit with a pen and write to heal, I grow.

1. What is one of my strengths?
2. Where do I need to grow?
3. What am I terrible at?
4. What makes me frustrated or tired?
5. What is the most important thing in my life?
6. Who are the most important people in my life?
7. How much sleep do I need?
8. What makes me feel stressed?
9. When do I feel relaxed?
10. What is my definition of success?
11. What type of worker am I?
12. How do I think others see me?
13. What makes me sad?
14. What makes me happy?
15. What makes me angry?
16. What do I value?
17. What type of friend do I want to be?
18. How do I describe what I do to others?
19. What things make me smile?
20. What makes me afraid of the future?

Take the time to answer these questions and learn the art of asking questions for growth. Don't be afraid; if people shut you down, then find some different people.

ASK GREAT QUESTIONS

Read Widely

My bedside table is full of books that often remain unread. A pile of reminders of what remains unfinished. Reading allows us the possibility to surrender to the power of story. Although my bedside contains many half read books, I continue to remind myself of the power of reading widely for a creative life.

Across this season I have been reading more fictional stories. I've been immersing myself in the stories of others. Worlds of imagination, sleeping places that need awakening, colours coming into spaces, the beauty of getting to know a character I will never meet and seeing their thoughts through the eyes of the narrator.

Each time I read, my heart and life grows.

Read a thousand books and your words will flow like a river. Lisa See

In a world that is consumed with quick, fast and cheap forms of entertainment, we forget easily the power of words colliding, ideas brewing and studying works from people who walked the earth in previous generations.

There is something very powerful about reading widely and allowing knowledge and growth to mark our rewards. Each week as my son goes to his exercise class, I make myself walk through the local library. I look out for spines with colours and shapes that call out my name.

Most of the Mums from the classes my children attend stand and talk in circles, and I sometimes wonder if they think I am running away out of fear. The truth is I seek out times each week to grow in my understanding of the power of story and myriad of words that sit in libraries awaiting discovery.

Words encourage more words. Our imagination is a powerful computer that grows when its muscle is flexed. We can train ourselves to read widely. We can grow in the marathon of focus to read our book to the very last page and breathe that sigh of relief when it is indeed done.

As well as reading more fiction novels this year, I have been on the journey of setting up a book club. A very simple gathering of women from different places to talk about a book we have chosen.

DEAR CREATIVE SELF

I have always dreamed of having a book club. I think from my teenage bedroom as I devoured Enid Blyton and 'The Babysitters Club' series. Sitting with a group of people and discussing the content, allows different opinions to brew across the atmosphere allowing strength to rise in diversity.

We read the same book across a month or so. Then we gather, with a glass of wine and a board full of cheese. We discuss what parts of the book we liked and what characters resonated with our imagination. Mostly I love that there is accountability in reading books that would mostly remain on my bedside table half finished.

Each night as my eyes tire towards closing, I read a few pages of my latest book, training myself to read every single day.

Reading grows our capacity as a storyteller.

Reading fills our hearts and lives with the power of narrative and the overcoming beauty of seasons across a lifetime.

Reading teaches our children to seek out wisdom from sages in our community.

Reading slows our hearts and lives from a constant stream of hustle and busyness.

This last year I set myself a goal of reading 50 books. That's nearly a book a week across the calendar year. Big books, short books and audio books make up this little goal I set.

Stretching my creative self towards discovery, hope and reading less on the Internet and holding paper in my hands.

How many books do you read across a year?

It is not about the number, it is about the growth of setting yourself accountable goals to grow and finish what lies within your reach.

Read widely creative one.

Each time you open up your mind to new ideas, collections of words and wisdom found in deep, quiet places, you grow. Life is lived, not consumed on a television. Passivity is imbedded in our culture. When we lean towards learning something new, there is activation in other parts of our lives.

The more we read, the greater we grow. Read widely and a catalogue of stories will follow you the rest of your life.

Dear Creative Self,

Somebody needs your story. When you surrender to the patience of turning page after page, your own story grows.

Stay home tonight. Turn off all technology, slow down and read a book. You can put a record on, build a fire and read till dawn.

You don't need to tell anyone, you can just discover the beauty of a story.

I know that distraction comes calling. The dishes in the sink and the guilt of what we should be doing. Let's slow down. Forget about what the world is doing and discover a universe within the pages of a novel.

Each page builds a library of words within our soul.

Each story asks us to empathize, think or laugh out loud.

Books are the playgrounds of our future endeavours and when we read widely it builds a scaffold of diversity for creativity.

Walk the library.

Borrow books from authors you know nothing of, with little expectation except to revel in the beauty of our imagination.

Learn lessons for your future.

Read, grow, learn and rest.

Yours truly,

Me

Creative Date

Todays date is to go to a library you wouldn't normally go to. Catch a train, drive across town and stay awhile.

Pack your lunch, sit on the couches and read on site.

Libraries are one of the foundation stones of our community. There are audio books, dvds and cookbooks; children's stories and puzzles ready to borrow.

Walk through the aisles and explore a little.

Pick up a genre you wouldn't normally read.

Sit and breathe in words.

Check out with a new collection and set yourself some accountability around reading.

Pioneering

"Writing is a powerful way to ignite those questions that can remain buried in places of shame and doubt. We will never find new answers, new directions and revelations unless we allow ourselves to question what has always been."

Be Curious

My little boy walked into my bedroom as the dawn was reaching across the sky, and he whispered, "Mum, what does being curious mean?"

My eyes half opened and squinted into his. I asked, "Where did you hear that word, buddy?"

He replied softly "My teacher said to me that I am a very curious little boy, and I was wondering if that is a bad thing?"

I sat up straight in bed, remembering. I allowed that feeling of dread to come over me as I knew what it was like to be labelled curious.

I was at a similar age as my little boy, when I'd snuck behind that backstage curtain, and made my way to the makeup table.

At all of six years old I'd covered myself in every colour of makeup I could find, not knowing that I was transforming myself into a clown and walking onstage to a scene that wasn't expecting that kind of entertainment.

Curiosity has always sat like a shame snake in my lap. Just like my son, who was wondering whether it is good or bad to live a life of curiosity.

Stories are captured in the hallways we walk down. However, culture, generational dialogues, pain and a whole myriad of life experience can hold us captive thinking that we should just stop asking, "Is there another way?"

Writing is a powerful way to ignite those questions that can remain buried in places of shame and doubt. We will never find new answers, new directions and revelations unless we allow ourselves to question what has always been.

There are secret sacred places where your questions and answers collide. These places can be unlocked through writing and discovery.

Be curious. Write to heal. Find the parts of your story that need to be recorded for the legacy of the coming generations.

Rather than giving everything we have to social media, what about digging deep into your story and writing to heal in your own life. Finding wisdom and thoughts, which are powerful, from our own story and brilliance.

Every time we do this, the reverberation across our life is powerful because when we discover transformation from our own stories, every person in our world is impacted.

The ripple effect of people who are not afraid to own their stories, change the narrative and then step out into their passion and purpose, is powerful.

You can do this, and all you need is a pen and a piece of paper.

I recently created an online writing course called Write Hard. Ernest Hemingway said it this way, "Write hard about the things that hurt".

The truth is, we have all been hurt, but there is power in those stories. Especially names that we have been called by teachers, or leaders— people who have thrown off the cuff statements that then become part of our identity.

I want to teach my little man that asking questions, being curious and pushing open doors of revelation that sit before us, is one of the best pursuits of a creative life.

There are revelations from these places that propel us into our glorious futures. We all have a story that can help another.

There is wisdom in our draws of revelation that can empower others. The voice that is discovered in the depths of our own narratives is awaiting expression. There is a beauty in searching out things that remain hidden.

> It is the glory of God to conceal things, but the glory of
> kings is to search things out. Proverbs 25:2 (NIV)

I think we were all born with the stamp of a King, desiring us to seek out wisdom. When was the last time you wrote with curiosity? We need to give ourselves permission to write imperfectly to find the gifts hidden beneath the rubble.

Journaling, memories and recording insight for your future self is a rhythm that awaits our discovery. Walking around museums, flicking through photo albums and asking the question, "Why?"

Write hard and long, my dear friend. It is a tool that will bring considerable growth and power into your future.

There is nothing wrong with asking a question that provokes thought. One that the book of Proverbs would tell us brings royalty and wisdom. Seek out those paths that lead to understanding and knowledge. Don't be afraid to seek and find. Look for the pilgrimage that is inviting you forward to rewrite this letter in your life.

Curiosity is in fact, one of the highest pursuits.

Dear Creative Self,

Let's remember to keep asking questions. Even those times when it is awkward and tough.

I am going to try to be more curious about the messages you are sending me. Allowing insight to speak loudly and the wisdom from within prevail.

Help me to slow enough to listen, to find the grace to begin and trust myself again.

I let go of the shame dialogues that hold me captive to the names that people have labelled across my life in places of the past.

Curiosity is our friend.

Let's seek out the gold of wisdom together.

Yours truly,

Me

DEAR CREATIVE SELF

Creative Date

Find a time this week to sit in silence or with instrumental music. Sit in a quiet spot and take the time to listen.

This is a very simple creative date for you today, but it is one of the most important tools as a creative artist, to get comfortable with listening rather than always speaking.

What emotions are present in your body as you sit with silence?

This is an opportunity to allow curiosity to guide you. Just begin by focusing on your breathing and be curious.

New Eyes

The plane landed and as I looked out of the small window I saw a curious mix of Asian architecture, European colours and mountains shadowing the horizon. It was an opportunity of a lifetime to go to the mountains of Nepal and see the work of an amazing aid organisation.

We were picked up in a small bus and my mouth was wide open as we drove the streets of Kathmandu in the aftermath of a huge earthquake. Tears streamed down my face as I saw cracks through century old buildings. I beckoned little children running the streets with woollen jumpers black with soot.

One of the reasons I love to travel is the crazy stories and people I find accompanying my suitcase. One of the greatest gifts we can give our creative self is to put ourselves in situations when we are not the ones in control.

When I travel overseas I sit and people watch, I overhear conversations and listen to people who have a completely different worldview than mine. If we sit around the same table, eating the same food with people who think like us, we will never stretch and grow the creative muscle that lies within. It is like I see the palette of the earth and its people with new eyes.

Before I had children travel was a huge part of my creative process. I've never flown business class; I've rarely stayed in 5 class hotels but still have the stories—the stories hiding in the slums, coffee shops and museums.

As a Mum now, I can't travel as often as I used to, but I've become committed to travelling my own city. I am determined to sit in places I've never been before, try cuisine from countries on my list to travel and experience theatre, comedy festivals and country pubs. I set myself creative dates weekly and as a family we have adventures planned to go places we have never been before.

Living an interesting life is less about the success of platforms given to us, the number of followers on our Social Media accounts or perceived influence we may long for. It is more about an interesting life that we explore, putting ourselves in the seat of the learner rather than the critic.

It's easy to be critical.

It's comfortable to stay home and watch Netflix.

DEAR CREATIVE SELF

It's safe to hang out with the same people day in and day out and not allow new people into our circles.

Libraries are playgrounds. Museums are story keepers. Swimming pools are our society secret holders. Markets are place makers. Beaches are village courts and we all have room in our backpacks for another tale. When was the last time you did something for the first time?

The new is waiting for our creative selves to grow into the fullness of our purpose. Our hearts were designed to be captivated. Your brain is a trampoline that was created to be stretched. These are my confessions of a serial people watcher.

Dear Creative Self,

There is more to our story. I know we have walked paths together that no one else knows about, but tomorrow a new adventure is waiting for you.

Go and gather new and interesting moments. Rather than having a perfect online life, I want you to have an interesting life full of people and new stories.

The stories that you gather have the capacity to leave a legacy of hope for those that follow.

Why don't you sit with people who think differently than you? I want you to find the time to forget what is happening. Instead of being overwhelmed with a fear of missing out, what if you get so lost in the possibility of adventures you are creating, that new wisdom, insight and creative pursuits pour out of space, time and refreshing is an integral part of the process of reflection.

See with new eyes.

Say yes to overseas trips, opening up places of discomfort and risk. Make appointments to visit places in your city, and pick up a camera to take photos on film.

Live a life that is interesting and wild. I'm so sorry for the times that I have allowed criticism to overtake you. It's time to tell fear to be gone and surrender to the potential of the new.

Where shall we go?

Yours truly,

Me

DEAR CREATIVE SELF

Creative Date

Today's creative adventure is to book a staycation in your own city. Find a friend or book it by yourself. Find a last minute discount, search out some deals and plan a city trip to explore.

Eat at restaurants you would never normally go to. Walk through the libraries, museums and bookshops.

Buy a roll of film and borrow a camera that only takes photos with film. Immerse yourself in the culture of your own city and ask yourself this simple question:

What inspires you?

Sleep in.

Drink five coffees.

Have an almond croissant.

Talk with a stranger.

Adventure is waiting.

Marred By Dust

The sun was rising on a new day and my eyes opened to the cool air of the New Zealand hinterlands. We had just flown in fresh from the snow of Queenstown where we ran a conference for church leaders from all over the world.

There was a sneaky moment as we were preparing the trip that my work colleague suggested that we go on a couple of day horse riding adventure to finish off the full work schedule. I had no idea what I was saying yes to.

I lay there in this wooden shack, knowing that the day to come was going to induce the soundtrack from the man from Snowy River. My three friends were amazing horse riders with lots of experience and I was the newbie, fresh from ten weeks of novice horse riding lessons. I had no idea what I had signed up for.

It is easy to watch a horse rider gallop through the countryside and assume that anyone can jump on and have a go. Then you add the wild hinterlands of New Zealand and the cold frost fresh from sub zero temperatures and it was no walk in the park. It was terrifying and exhilarating, all together wild.

I was a terrible horse rider during that short trip through the mountains and yes I had to keep up with my very competent friends. I could not walk the next day and I wanted to give up but I was on the horse. I was in my own story, rather than on the sidelines, watching someone else live theirs.

We are a consuming society. We watch people play sport instead of getting in the arena ourselves. We screen binge people making food and then order take away. We consume worship songs online forgetting that we haven't sung ourselves. We scroll through the opinions of others and wonder why we feel conflicted often.

Creativity is not for the elite few it is for everyone. The way that we speak to our creative self, about what we fear the most matters. Each time we criticize someone else for their failing courage when they are marred with dust in the arena, we forget that we actually are the one sitting in the grandstands watching.

Theodore Roosevelt orated this over one hundred years ago:

> *It is not the critic who counts; not the man who points out how the strong man stumbles, or where the doer of deeds could have*

done them better. The credit belongs to the man who is actually in the arena, whose face is marred by dust and sweat and blood; who strives valiantly; who errs, who comes short again and again, because there is no effort without error and shortcoming.

Did I feel ridiculous on the back of that wild horse?

Was I scared out of myself every mountain we climbed?

A huge, resounding yes! I did fall off the horse as we went around a corner and my jumper hooked on a low-lying branch that flung me to the forest floor. I had no choice but to get back on the horse. We were hours away from our settlement and I learned just as much in getting back on, as I did in the moment of victory when we came to the end of our ride.

It is so easy to sit in the seat of the critic, with our keyboard at our fingertips, and tell everyone else how bad the players of the team are doing. What if we got in the game though? When we face our greatest fears of failure, defeat and embarrassment we win, every time.

The dance of our creative self is one of movement and momentum. When we criticize others rather than having a go ourselves, it becomes the greatest area of stagnation in our creative pursuits.

The credit belongs to those who are actually having a go. Marred with dust, falling off their proverbial horses and getting back on again.

Dear Creative Self,

Remember that time when you used to do crazy things, like learning to scuba dive off the coast of Indonesia and snow boarding down the white powder of Queenstown. The feeling of risk and emancipation from the ordinary in your everyday was thrilling.

You are designed to live with wild abandonment and every time that you experience new environments the memory banks of your expression swell.

Thank you for getting in the arena and allowing dust to mark your mind. It is easy to criticize those who are having a go.

Comparing your everyday with their latest pursuits. What if though, you created a life that was interesting, and that you stand alongside others rather than pull them down for their perceived failure?

Book that trip you have always wanted to go on. Visit that Nature Park, waterfall or dam. Shall we go camping sometime soon?

Even though you don't love the discomfort, the thrill of waking with a chill in the air and not worrying about whether your clothes are ironed or not is worth it. When you jump in the arena, exploring the depth and width of your potential, you grow.

Your creative expression rises when you fill your tank with the highs and lows of just having a go. It may not be something you enjoy in the moment, but as you look back with tears in your eyes, you will remember the pure joy of trying something new.

Let's stop criticizing others and start failing forward.

Yours truly,

Me

Creative Date

Today your creative date is all about discovering something for the first time. What if you booked a horse riding afternoon or a swim with dolphins?

Is there something wild you have always wanted to do, but continue to sit in the grandstands watching others?

This is an opportunity to book that community team sport or to invite a group of friends hiking and stay overnight in a forest with limited phone reception.

It's time to search through the parts of our lives where we criticize others. We can now take a walk in their shoes to the arena. It is one where we are very likely to fail but the stretch it will bring to our creative selves will be palpable.

Take More Risks

We went shopping for something specific: school shoes. My son became fixated on a pair of shoes that didn't really match my idea of what was uniform code, plus they were a size too big, with no smaller options.

A meltdown was ensuing on both sides of the shoe fence, with my toddler slowly pulling anything within reach off the shelves.

We were one month into launching our new business, a surf brand, and we had just booked a last minute trip to New Zealand. My patience was thin from the pain of growth and dreams realised. Actually, I was regretting taking the risk of something new.

Have you ever had those days? Full of regret.

Days with those emotional hangover feelings, thinking *what have we done*?

You know when you realise that your friends and family are asking the same question without whispering the words out loud.

Pioneering the dreams in your heart is not for the faint-hearted. It is easy to come up with ideas but to have the courage to take the risk and have a go? *That* is next level faith.

Back to the shops and our school shopping expedition and what happened next. My husband grabbed a pillow with an inspirational quote on it. When we got home, I rolled my eyes. There are some days when another quote is just not what I need.

The pillow said this: "If you dream big enough, anything can come true."

I sat on our bed and wanted to throw the pillow out of our window. A pioneering life can be so annoying.

We need to be ready to have the courage to take risks, along with wisdom to take the steps necessary to live the life you have dreamed of.

Real courage takes great risks.

The future does not belong to the timid, it belongs to the brave. Ronald Regan

DEAR CREATIVE SELF

Every day that I see that pillow sitting on the chair in the corner of our lounge room, it is a reminder to my soul asking me to take heart and courage to step into the brilliance of God's plans for our future.

> *Commit your work to the Lord, and your plans will be established. Proverbs 16: 3 (NIV)*

Committing our work to God means actually doing something with it. Step out with the courage to dream bravely my friends. Take risks and have the courage to actually act today on the dreams that have been lying dormant.

What work is it time for your creative self to commit to?

Pick up that manuscript.

Type that blog.

Put on those exercise clothes.

Step into the great unknown.

Pull out that camera.

Write that book proposal.

Send an email to that person.

Step forward with what you have in your hands today, even if it is very, very small.

Take a risk and do something you have never done before. Be bold and courageous, and your future self will thank you.

TAKE MORE RISKS

Dear Creative Self,

Let's take a risk and do something we have never done before.

The possibility of stepping into the great unknown is so powerful; pioneering the ideas and possibilities that we often speak of together.

What if together we believed the small voice of God within, and began to take steps towards the ideas that are held deep within our souls?

Thankyou for the times that you have allowed new spaces and places to bring great reward.

The greatest risk we can take is to be truly heard and seen.

I'm all in.

Yours truly,

Me

Creative Date

Today's task is to do something that is completely out of character for you. Sign up for a creative class that scares you, like a pottery class or a painting workshop.

Take a creative risk.

Maybe it's a public speaking mastermind or a comedy routine in an open mic night at a local club.

When we take creative risks it challenges and changes us.

To grow in creativity we need to try things we have never done before.

Accountability clause:

Maybe you could post about it on social media as well, so you follow through.

And, I'm going now.

Bye.

Get Feedback

Corporate environments thrive on the performance evaluation system. Recently I was teaching a marketing workshop for the government and as I collected the feedback survey forms I felt my anxiety rise.

I quickly shoved the papers in my briefcase and told myself to breathe slowly. The leftovers in my heart from those meetings with performance evaluation papers held in hand, reminded me of high school examinations and the art of trying too hard.

Feedback can be thrilling for some but for others it brings with it sheer terror. As a creative I want to grow, and I also want to see the things that my own pain shadows in my life. Self-awareness is muddy water that helps us grow in productivity and life.

It is not an easy space however. After twenty years of public speaking, I still have to calm myself as I read feedback on the risks I have just taken. Learning to listen to learn, rather than respond is one of the greatest growth spaces. We need to be both kind to ourselves, and at the same time open to hear what can feel overwhelmingly critical.

Maturity helps us to gain our identity not from people, but our own set of life values. The words that people speak of our creativity though, can be a bitter pill to swallow.

How are you going in the area of feedback on your creativity?

Is it easy for you to accept or is it difficult and you retreat?

Without feedback, we can stay stagnant. Every writer needs an editor to shine light on the words we carry deep within our hearts. A songwriter needs a producer to hear sounds that they cannot hear in their own voice. Event coordinators need to hear of the experience of their audience, as they made their way through the crowd.

There are stories that we need to hear, even when it feels like an army coming against us. Stand true in the promises of our days gone by and remember the identity and values that shape our lives.

DEAR CREATIVE SELF

We all are on a journey of becoming. There is always a place in our leadership, creativity and lives that can change. Feedback draws us into places of growth. This stretch is not an easy one, but the possibility of sitting without defense and allowing the perception of others to help us understand our craft even more, is worth it.

Getting feedback can be as simple as asking for a mentor to give you feedback on your current season. When we ask someone further ahead of us to give us some advice or wisdom, we need to then learn to listen.

If there is something that erupts inside our hearts and lives as we listen to the conversation that comes a little close to home, it is a great time to reframe where we get our sense of identity.

Do you get your courage from your creative craft?

Do you get your self worth from the number of followers you have online?

When we hear someone say something truthful, yet difficult, it is easy to push back, get defensive and maybe get angry. I am learning that creativity is a very sensitive field to receive feedback on.

As I read through the feedback sheets from my workshop, I find I need a little time to come back to it with perspective, when I am not still reeling in the aftermath of putting myself out there. I need space between my expression of creativity and the lesson found in the feedback. After a while, I sit with the feedback and find ways to implement small steps of growth.

Rather than repeating the feedback over and over allowing it to stunt my growth in pain, I need to find ways to unpack the feedback with courage. I sit with a good friend and ask their opinions on my work. I seek wise counsel from someone who I trust, who will tell the truth but also help me to create some scaffold around the feedback.

A great idea is to listen for reoccurring feedback, rather than a one off scattergun approach. Across a season of life, I find ways to look out for regular feedback that is reoccurring. Finding ways to sit in the discomfort of the light shining on our weak parts and stepping into the great possibility of change can be difficult.

It can also be very sobering. We can feel vulnerable and unsafe, but what is even worse is having boulders that stand in the way of our personal growth and development.

Each time I sit and allow people I trust to speak into my life, bringing wisdom, perspective and insight, great shifts and transitions are instigated in my everyday life.

Do you feel a little stuck?

Maybe it is time to recalibrate your defense mechanisms around feedback and invite accountability into your creative arena. You could sit with a coach or a mentor. You could ask someone a series of questions and then listen to their honest answers. This takes courage and trust but it is an amazing space of momentum.

GET FEEDBACK

Make friends with feedback.

Sit comfortably with honest conversations.

And lean into those stories that bring up your defenses, finding ways to lay them down to learn again.

Dear Creative Self,

I know that hearing people talk about your creative pursuits can be rough. When you have put your heart and soul into the ideas, it's hard to hear that someone thinks you could change or grow.

I know there are blocks that stop you from growing. There are narratives and stories that you are telling yourself that hold you tight in a pattern of safety.

You want to grow now though. Find ways to connect deeply with people who have your back. Listen to feedback not as a personal criticism but an opportunity of growth.

Find a way not to take feedback so personally, and hold your ideas lighter. Know that listening to the right people, not everyone, brings great reward. You're not throwing your ideas out to the crowd to give feedback but bringing closer a small group of people who understand to give you some insight.

What if you promised to not be so sensitive and play sentences over and over in our minds?

Surrender to the beauty of a greater tomorrow.

You are not defined by what you create or do; those who love you despite your craft celebrate you. There are those who have seen your very best and worst, yet love you still.

You have known your share of heartache in the area where criticism has muted your sense of worth and security. Today is an opportunity to recalibrate back to the original design and your first love.

God loves you no matter what you bring.

He is faithful to help and come alongside.

Yours truly,

Me

Creative Date

Today's creative date is to set a mentoring appointment with someone about your creative craft. This can be a paid appointment with a coach or a coffee with someone in your field that has some insight into your artistic life and can bring perspective.

Come ready with questions to ask them to give you feedback and insight. These five questions may be a great start:
1. In what areas can you see that I need to grow?
2. In the midst of my online spaces can you see anything that you'd like to share where there might be a lack of authenticity?
3. What do you think is holding me back from growing personally?
4. What seasons have you grown the most in your life?
5. What distractions have you cut out of your life, to pursue your craft?

This is a simple list of questions, but honestly it could be a simple conversation about growth, weakness and strength. Find ways to recalibrate and trust the authenticity between you. Try to lay your defenses down and just listen.

Spirituality and a Sense of Purpose

"Solitude. The sacred. These are the paths that no one can walk except you. A conversation with our Creator, where He reminds us that the desire we hold in the cradle of our hearts was put there for Him."

Nurtured By the Sea

I swam from the turquoise shallows into the navy deep. Hoping that each stroke would wash away the discomfort that had become my friend. Some days don't need words to describe the myriad of emotion; some days need the multifaceted reflection of the sea.

The sandy beaches I grew up on, the ones I escaped school to build sandcastles and dune bunkers over, have become the balm of healing that my adult heart required.

There is a small black notebook that sits on my bedside. It has been my companion now for near on twenty years. The elastic that used to sit firmly around its cover now hangs loosely, worn by time. A small biro pen drawing denotes a time longer than my body can remember when I drew a simple sketch of the sea and a scribbled note alongside.

'The healing balm of the sea.'

The ocean has not always been a place of healing, since I sat on its shores watching one of my best friend's surfboards floating out to sea, saying goodbye to him after his funeral. There are also hidden parts of the beaches that hold secrets and memories that I no longer want to remember.

The sea however in the midst of its memories, has taught me a few lessons that have deeply brought the rhythm of healing into my today.

Yesterday's tide is just like yesterday's paper.

Yesterday's newspaper found on the bottom of pot plants—what is so present and hurtful today can easily be washed away by the tide of a new day. The ocean has taught me in the midst of its endless story that tides come and go. Despite the pain of what happened in the past, finding a rhythm of letting go and beginning again is an essential healing place in the arms of the ocean.

Everything you need to survive can be found in its depths. The nurturing your soul desires is found in these simple places.

We often go out searching for another answer, another formula or someone to rescue our healing. However, as I come close to a decade of living back by the ocean, I realise everything we need is found in the depths. Your depth, your story and your capacity can be as deep and wide as the ocean that covers the earth. Wide and wavering, everything you need to survive is deep within your soul.

Some days we need to drop everything and tell no one and stare off into the ocean. We need to learn to nurture ourselves. Turning inward to the pain that holds us captive, unpack the emotion and recreate the safety that we each need.

It's like an endless novel—the ocean and its breadth is a secret place of knowing that holds all our conversations deep within its fold. In a culture that is constantly telling us to shout out our worth to the multitudes, the ocean calls us to a place of comfort nestled within the quiet.

Summer, winter, autumn and spring all bring different hues and possibility. We can just run away on occasion. Go to the sea and not tell anyone. Ever. Sit within its chasm. Swim within its endless simplicity and recover. Nurture our hearts and soul.

One day recently I had swum from the shallows into the deep. I was contemplating the complexity of losing my dear friend way too soon. As I swam so far that the land was starting to fade, in the midst of unfathomable beauty, a small bright orange monarch butterfly came and sat on my salty nose. I started to tread water completely perplexed by this seeming contrast within nature and was unsure what to do with its meaning.

I decided not to choose comfort. I chose to nurture my soul, accepting and acknowledging the deep pain of this loss.

That no matter how far away we try to run, no matter the distance of loneliness and confusion that awakens us at night, we are never too far from the shore, for butterflies to come and land on our noses. Once again on that obscure summer's afternoon, I remembered the whisper from the decade before.

'The healing balm of the sea.'

With the perfect combination of making us feel so very small, wild and blue all at once. Take me away to the sea. With a sandwich, starfish and maybe a coffee tucked in the side. And let's tell no one ever. (Not even Instagram)

May the insight you are seeking, find you waiting on the shores of the sea. As we learn to nurture those stories in our creative hearts that do not add up, we allow the highs and lows of life to shape the depth and height of our creative selves.

NURTURED BY THE SEA

Dear Creative Self,

Let's run away to the sea. Immersed in nature and leaving the tension of the day in the sandy shores. Let's lay your burdens down in the ocean of relief.

Laying down those things that no longer fit in your today. Clothes that used to fit, they were comforting and we could hide behind them.

What if you reset your capacity within the depths of the sea?

Creation has a power that is often ignored because it reminds us of how small we are. Surrender to the power of anonymity. Remind yourself of the millions of people that have walked along the shore.

Shall we run away to the sea?

Pick up seashells and feel the earth beneath your feet.

Walk, rumbling with the stories that you can't explain.

Allow the presence of the Creator God to come in close, showing us his wonderful artwork once again.

Shall we?

Yours truly,

Me

Creative Date

Today's creative exercise is to take a little notebook to the sea. If you are far from the ocean, find a screen saver or photo of the ocean and load it up on your computer.

Bring with you some coloring in pencils or a little tray of watercolor paints.

Today you are going to draw the ocean in front of you. Notice the different hues of blue, green and brown. Start to scribble, colour, draw or paint.

Look out upon the horizon again and draw.

Look up into nature and allow its magnitude to overwhelm you.

Draw in your little notebook.

Discover the hues, tones and beauty as a canvas that draws you into a new narrative and story.

Take the time to draw.

For no one else, except the sheer beauty of looking, noticing and creating.

Rhythm and Grace

I crave routine. I also love spontaneous crazy adventures. The art of showing up to a blank page and beginning again is a discipline that constantly is a pain in my rear!

My day often begins with intense dreaming. The time between the darkness of dawn and the light of early morning is a time that my brain flows into a deep dream state. I have never been great in the morning as I think my body is recovering from the intensity of its morning sleep filled movie.

Our children jump on my bed to wake me in the morning and I have not needed an alarm clock now ever since becoming a Mother. I tumble out of bed and make my way to the coffee machine.

As the coffee wakes my taste buds, I begin to unravel to the day and desire clarity of purpose for the moment. If I am honest I often grab my phone and scroll, or some days I write deep and meaningful passages provoked by that first coffee hit.

The times that I really get into a rhythm of grace are those times when I put the most important things first. Holding my children in a hug for a little longer than required. A prayer that surrenders my day to being lead by my Maker, rather than self made. Sitting on our terrace with a warm cup and my Bible.

When my days are shaped by the meaningful and purpose filled, it completely changes my outcome. Lately I have been trying to walk around the block or do exercise at my gym before I pick up a phone.

These scaffolds and boundaries completely change the way I speak to my creative self. I was designed with the need for scaffold to create purpose, and when these foundations are strong, it really helps me to create with intention.

We all crave routine. Our earth is imbued with routine. Each day the night cloaks our day with darkness and every morning the sun awakes with the dawn. Each spring, flowers blossom and every autumn the trees shed their leaf clothes.

As I sit and watch the wildlife in my little seaside town, I am aware of their daily routine as well. The willie wagtails that squawk waiting for dusk to envelope them and the pelicans that fly in formation towards their island home.

DEAR CREATIVE SELF

This poem from ancient biblical texts helps me find perspective around grace and rhythm.

> Are you tired? Worn out? Burned out on religion? Come to me. Get away with me and you'll recover your life. I'll show you how to take a real rest. Walk with me and work with me—watch how I do it. Learn the unforced rhythms of grace. I won't lay anything heavy or ill fitting on you. Keep company with me and you'll learn to live freely and lightly. Matthew 11: 28-30 (MSG)

The rhythm of grace that we all seek is not an impotent one. It is just one filled with more intention. We were created for routine. If you are without routine, it is very likely that you will feel creatively unsatisfied. When we work every moment of the waking day, we begin our days with our phones and end the day with a screen, binging a Netflix show, we loose sight of the natural rhythm that calls us into its company. It is a place of freedom and flexibility.

It is a rhythm of grace.

Creative routines can become stale and unforgiving quickly. My creative self gets bored very quickly and it's a fine line between the scaffold that I require and a recalibration to suit the season. Every New Year, I take the time to go on a personal retreat away from screens and opinion to find the scaffold that I need for the coming season. Often this process is very painful, because I need to say no to some things that were great, but no longer hold a grace for the coming year.

Each year I set goals and routines that unpack the season past and lean into the wisdom for the new.

This year I made these changes to my daily routine. A phone black out from 7pm in the evening, a 10pm bedtime, a 7am wake up time, a 8am exercise slot.

These simple diary appointments speak to my creative self by creating a scaffold for my mental, emotional and spiritual health.

How is your routine?

Is it one shaped by grace?

When we block out time for creativity, we make space for tech free times. What about prayer becoming fulcrum points of our schedules and plans?

Your schedule could include moments for weekly family connection, exercise and journaling to help us heal. These parts of our scaffold bring a rhythm of grace that we all crave.

I love the words of Jesus, paraphrased by Eugene Petersen, when he talks about bringing all that is heavy and full of burden and laying it down at the feet of Jesus. When we create moments of release that are a part of our regular routine, it completely changes that way that we lean into the new.

Dear Creative Self,

What are you doing habitually that is making you tired? Maybe it's the phone sitting on your bedside table. It could be those late nights scrolling photos of other people's creative pursuits.

What if you made a scaffold to help you have a rhythm that is manageable?

Thank you for always having a go when you create a new rule or regulation in your schedule. For always being willing to try again each time you stuff it up.

What parts of your daily schedule need to change for your health?

I'm sorry for the times that I have demanded more of you than what you have to give. When you have stayed up late and then booked in appointments from early in the morning. Those seasons when you haven't given yourself the space to recover and begin again.

When food has become a comfort rather than a fuel and your friends became background whilst I surfed screens in their presence.

You're ready to lay it all down and begin again.

Shall we create a landscape with some new rules?

Knowing there will be times when you just want to grab your phone, eat takeaway and stay up late. Start again. Let's look for some new habits and possibilities that create a rhythm of grace.

Yours truly,

Me

Creative Date

Grab a massive piece of paper and some coloured marker pens. We are going to create a scaffold for your creative week that includes some important spheres for your weekly rhythm.

Start with the schedule of your everyday habits.

Write the time between waking up and eating breakfast. Make a scaffold that will help you to develop a daily routine that begins the day well. The way we start a day, intensely impacts the whole.

Do you want to pray silently before getting out of bed?

What time do you want to get up each day?

What time are you allocating for exercise?

When would you like to pick up your phone?

Then jump to the end of the day. Create a routine for the closing of your day. Even a simple habit like going to bed at the same time each night, how late you can drink caffeine, listening to a sleep meditation or reading before falling asleep can really help you find a rhythm of grace.

Now turn over the page and draw out a weekly schedule. It is time to put in journaling, your work schedule, time for fun, family and friends. You can put in a weekly creative date so you can explore your city. Time to work on future projects. This becomes the scaffold that helps you say yes to other people's agenda for your life with wisdom.

Share your new scaffold with a friend, life coach, pastor or partner for accountability.

Liminal

There are many moments across the seasons of my life that I have longed for clarity. There have been those times when I've wished for the steps to be simple and clear, but often answers I am seeking are not answered in formulas like our culture produces on demand; I have found through times of great unknowing that God calls me into the spaces in-between.

Our culture delights in showing us places of arrival and destination, but I have found the seeking spaces, the liminal spaces are those that God is drawing us to. Across my life I have found these places, these moments in-between, have always been the places that we see dimly.

For now we see in a mirror dimly, but then face to face. Now I know in part; then I shall know fully, even as I have been fully known.

1 Corinthians 13:12 (ESV)

The Liminal Space is an artistic phrase used to describe the space when you are on the threshold of something new and wonderful, but you are just not there yet. It's the 'in-between.'

We spend most of our days in seasons of transition, than we actually do in seasons of success—so how come we feel so ashamed of describing our days this way?

I love this idea of threshold. 'The magnitude or intensity that must be exceeded for a certain reaction, phenomenon, result, or condition to occur or be manifested.'

My definition is this...

We are destined for lives of passion and purpose, but we are called to a waiting position of hope.

What I'm learning about the Liminal Space (the moments right at the threshold of new) is that we can so easily lose the potency of these precious moments by filling our time with just anything, rather than the right things. I believe the space between the known and the unknown teaches us more than any opportunity does. It can feel dark, lonely and unsure, because we are leaning towards places we have never been before. It is easy to rely on our old experiences of what God has done, but what if he is leading us to the in-between, through the Liminal Space, to something we have never known before?

One of my favourite writers Richard Rohr says this of the Liminal Space:

A unique spiritual position where human beings hate to be but where the biblical God is always leading them. It is when you have left the tried and true, but have not yet been able to replace it with anything else. It is when you are finally out of the way. It is when you are between your old comfort zone and any possible new answer. If you are not trained in how to hold anxiety, how to live with ambiguity, how to entrust and wait, you will run… anything to flee this terrible cloud of unknowing.

Are you willing to say no to some things, so you can say yes to a place of clarity and calling but it is often a space of unknowing?

Unlearning.

Unleashing.

Revealing.

Are you happy to walk slowly in an open space of transition, rather than fill your days with something, anything, to flee the terrible cloud of unknowing?

This is the walk of the in-between.

To keep hoping, to keep discovering, to keep dreaming—but often we see these places dimly.

Beauty is awaiting discovery in the in-between.

LIMINAL

Dear Creative Self,

There are moments where the in-between is the last place on earth you want to be. Stepping out and doing something new can be the scariest place on earth.

You have come so far though. There have been moments in the past where you had no idea where you were going. You were frozen in fear, stuck in those places of darkness and shadows.

Then a door opens, a new conversation, a place of freedom—cracked open by a random chance encounter. There is always purpose in the spaces that we are led to in the liminal.

You don't have to always have it all together. Not knowing can actually be the greatest of adventures.

Being unsure is okay.

Seeing grey where there used to be technicolour, can just be a season not a destination.

Lean towards clarity.

Find spaces where you are not in control, you are not the boss, you are not the captain of the ship.

Sit back and allow the journey to take you along and notice the flowers on the side of the road.

Open your eyes to the luminous, the strange and the humble places that your feet walk upon.

The oceans push and pull at His command and as we surrender to the turning of a new season we see that He was always drawing us home.

The unclear in our life is not to be feared; in fact, we cannot step into the new, without walking through the unknown.

Yours truly,

Me

Creative Date

Today's date is to go and watch a movie without anyone else. Choose a film you wouldn't normally watch and surrender to the power of trying something new.

Grab a coffee, buy your favourite treat and surrender.

Sit and immerse yourself in the great power of someone else's story.

You could go to a new cinema, sit in the lounge and people watch.

Step into places that make you feel a little uncomfortable and do something that you have never done before.

Notice who else in is the cinema with you, look around and explore the room. Write a story in your mind about what they did this morning before they arrived in this same liminal space as you.

Turn off your phone, mark your diary as busy and step into a simple space of in-between.

The Sacred Secret Place

The sacred in my life is my source of inspiration. We live in a world that focuses on the external: we watch the highlight reels and we allow desire to run rampant in our hearts.

Desire was foundational to the redemption of humankind. If you believe there is a story beyond the story of this moment, then you come to a place of reckoning in the midst of desire.

Yesterday my daughter found five dollars under her pillow from her first tooth falling out. In our house the first tooth bounty is five dollars and from then on it drops to whatever we can find on the floor of the car.

As we walked through the shopping centre, I heard the coins she received that morning clanging in her pocket. Everywhere we went yesterday she was insistent. "Mum can we go to the shops?" "Mum, how far to the shops?" "Mum I need to spend my money!"

The treasure in her pocket was unravelling her desire to buy something new. Oh, the delight of a new toy, lip-gloss or lollies.

I see that same desire in my own heart over and over. Each and every time I scroll through your screens the desire ignites and somehow I believe the lie—that one more pair of shoes, a holiday or a new pen will fulfil the deep longings in my heart.

We were created with desire. There is nothing wrong with surrendering to the potential of wanting more. However in my life, I am learning that when I allow that desire to be filled with the sacred it completely changes the way I step into my tomorrow.

When we desire what others have, instead of rumble with our own stories it becomes a place of shallow comfort. Just like our hunger pains are to remind us that we haven't eaten. Our heart has pangs that create a longing for something more.

In your heart of hearts do you desire something more of your life?

My answer to this perplexing question is digging and developing a sacred secret place. There are secret questions: there are places that my heart has delved, that you will know nothing about.

The authenticity clause of our online culture does not mean that we lose the beauty of living a quiet and surrendered life. A life that unpacks the pain, the longing and desire in places away from the public eye.

Vulnerability is not about a public showing of the hurt and stories that have plagued our lives. It is the capacity to surrender to the process of growth, as wisdom is unearthed in those places of quiet.

> If I find in myself a desire, which no experience in this
> world can satisfy, the most probable explanation is
> that I was made for another world. CS Lewis

Solitude. The sacred. These are the paths that no one can walk except you. A conversation with our Creator, where He reminds us that the desire we hold in the cradle of our hearts was put there for Him. In conclusion, those desires show us that we were made for more.

1 John 2:17 (NIV) says it this way: The world and its desires pass away, but whoever does the will of God lives forever.

How can we know what the will of God is for our lives?

It is found in those secret, sacred places. These paths are when we walk through forests of opinion, judgement and pain. The times that we reference our beliefs and belonging by the sages of days gone by. Where we sit in the seat of the learner rather than having to be the one on the stage.

Success is reformed in these places by the ache of belonging to a world beyond our today. Our goal should be to leave a legacy of hope that is framed by eternity rather than our success. This is a hope that speaks so deeply to our soul that we were named before the earth was even formed.

Our identity is not shaped by the external. Success is not experienced through the amount in our bank account, but the depth of our souls.

Fame will never satisfy the longings of your heart. Being known across the world only magnifies your pain rather than heals it. Each and every time we surrender to the discomfort of sitting in the sacred, we grow.

Growth is not easy, but it is satisfying. It is satisfying to look back over our own stories and see that we have surrendered to the stretch of the sacred, and developed depth and humility.

This is the sacred in my life. These are the places I cannot show you or give you. You cannot take my sacred away from me. You can copy my ideas, you can try to mimic my voice but the sacred secret places cannot be replicated.

They are His and mine alone.

THE SACRED SECRET PLACE

Dear Creative Self,

There is a sacred secret place that only you have travelled. It is a quiet space of peace, calm and presence. The creative parts of your life are those parts that cannot be copied by another.

They are the early morning prayers, whispered as you have tried to counsel the doubts that have crept in. They are the moments of courage when you have spoken your thoughts and wondered if anyone in the room understands. They are moments of unbelief, those times of sheer exhaustion and times when He has carried you further than you believed you could ever have gone.

Those sacred secret places, when you have allowed time and space to stand still and then tried again. When you have fought the voices in your head that scream you will never be enough, have enough or do all those things in your heart.

It comes in the boundaries that you have set, when someone wants to take the very little time that you hold vulnerably in your hands. It's the times when you say no again, the times when you choose to let go and smile for no reason at all.

Then moments of grace and reminding yourself how far you have travelled. When you have forgiven those who take so much and remember that the original design of humanity was to be emptied so that you can be filled again.

Choose to keep giving. Even though you feel tired and unsure whether you have anything else in your tank. The art of surrender is giving what you have so that you can be filled again.

When you are emptied, there is more room to grow again.

Yours truly,

Me

Epilogue: the letter of our life

I remember years ago driving on a freeway with the entire contents of my bedroom jammed into my car. Two weeks prior, I had encountered clarity in a way that is hard to describe. I had an encounter that was life changing and it directly impacted the trajectory of my life.

I was standing at the back of a church with my arms crossed, not interested in the service that was taking place. I thought it was weird and I had no intention of entering into the songs being sung.

I was disconnected, and if I was really honest the letter being written of my life then would have ended in heartache. I was dating a boy who took me on cycles of emotional abuse. I was on a rollercoaster of self-doubt about my life and its purpose. I was overwhelmed by an eating disorder and my parents had recently divorced after twenty years of marriage. One of my closest friends had taken his life by suicide and I was desperate for a new beginning.

The sad thing is this: no one knew any of these stories. Everyone thought I was totally winning the race of life. I had my own business, teaching hundreds of children dance and drama. I won a place at the most prestigious university in our city and I was on sold out stages acting in professional musical theatre.

I stood at the back of that room thinking if only they knew the real me. My arms crossed as a defence mechanism to keep the truth contained.

Then gradually I let my arms drop down and I began to be truly honest with myself. I allowed an awakening from the depth of my being to take over. I lifted my arms and surrendered to the possibility of a new letter being written. Someone spoke words over my life that made me believe I could be honest and let out all the stories I was carrying by myself.

> God rewrote the text of my life when I opened the book
> of my heart to his eyes. Psalm 18: 24 (MSG)

I went home that night and packed up my bedroom, with as many belongings I could fit in my car and I drove to the city to begin again. I drove on that freeway with music blaring and tears streaming down my face. Then in a shock moment the whole front window of my car smashed into pieces, for no particular reason. It was like hundreds of little circles became the one piece of glass that used to be the clear glass of my car's front window.

The decision I made to show up to my story with complete honesty, seemed to be shifting things in the atmosphere that I don't know how to describe.

I was breaking a forcefield in my life in the unseen. I'd made a decision and I followed through with its consequences, I gave up my business and I began again. This time, walking hand in hand with the Author of my life, opening my heart up with honesty and transparency for the possibility of a better tomorrow.

I learnt that letting go of my old life was necessary to step into my new story for tomorrow.

It is time for us to get honest about the way that we speak to our creative selves to bring about change and transformation. Being honest, like brutally honest, with oneself is a powerful tool of transformation.

> *For we are his workmanship, created in Christ Jesus*
> *for good works, which God prepared beforehand, that*
> *we should walk in them. Ephesians 2:10 (NIV)*

The beauty of this awakening that happened in my life is that I didn't have to face the complexity of my creative life alone anymore. I found this partnership grow in the workmanship of the life that was being authored together with my God.

This word workmanship when you look back to the Greek origin of the word it is this word *poiema* which expresses the fullness of our life as a work of art expressed as a poem. I have found ever since that moment of complete honesty, that my life is being authored as well as being written everyday. The words of our life are being chosen carefully, written as an epic work of art together with the Creator of the Universe.

Your life is a letter.

There is perfection found in the stories that hide within the chapters of your story. Yes, there are also many hard stories and times of darkness and despair but together as we write with a God who created our innermost being, we see the beauty of creativity not being a curse but an expression of the fullness of who we were created to be.

The letter of your life is important.

The stories that enhance the hues, tones and colours may seem inconsequential but they are so necessary.

No one has ever lived the story that is your life. It is a work of art, and when partnered together with the meta story of humanity it starts to make sense.

EPILOGUE: THE LETTER OF OUR LIFE

Write the story of your life dear creative one, in a way that brings hope and light to those who encounter it.

Bring honesty to those hard places and learn to grow with your questions, rather than get stuck in disappointment and discouragement. This is your one, wild, irreplaceable manuscript of a life.

What letter are you writing to your future?

Dream

I woke up in the midst of a dream of reading glasses being cleaned.

It was a cold morning with a mist of opportunity awaiting the present of the day. An old soul picked up a pair of tiger rimmed glasses and breathed heavily on the lens.

A heave of air blurred the looking glass so that it was filled with a mist of grey. Then with ease of knowing the man rubbed the glass clean.

In that one moment, I saw a movement of clarity coming across the seekers on the earth. Moments of presence, opportunities captured and the writers, the critics, the seers and mystics—they arose.

> *"All ye writers and critics who prophesy with their pen. Keep your eyes wide as the time won't come again."* Bob Dylan

There is something special in this present moment in history. My dream bought such deep inspiration as I awoke from my slumber.

Clarity is coming, my creative friend. Vision to see what has been hidden. Moments of awakening that were designed for those who see.

Those who are walking around lost in their thoughts. Moments of perfect synergy, where the words you have been hoping will come, will flood like a waterfall from another place. Another time.

> *Then their eyes were opened, and they recognised [Jesus]. Luke 24:31 (NRSV)*

An awakening of words and purpose is coming. A filling of direction and moments of courage that will never come again. So gather the prophets, the writers and those who long to see again.

Clarity is coming, in fact, she is already here.

Acknowledgements

To my family...

Thankyou for believing in my crazy ideas. Charl, Maximus and Liberty you are my world!

To my writing gang...

You know who you are, thankyou for the prayers, encouragement and friendship.

To my circle of women...

You are my kin.

To my publishing powerhouse...

Rachelle Dusting front cover artist, Kellie Book Design and Em Hazeldean my editor, thanks for your courage and belief.

And lastly...

To every person who supports writers and buys our books, especially my loyal readers, thankyou from the bottom of my heart, you make dreams come true.

Print is not dead!

Endorsements

Amanda Viviers strikes again! In Dear Creative Self, Amanda leads you on a personal journey to not only discovering your unique voice but sharing it. You will think this book is written by God just for you as each page nurtures you through the process of connecting with your most authentic self. Amanda holds nothing back as she allows you in her sanctuary. Her vulnerability is a personal encouragement diary reminding you that even in the most challenging times "you are not alone". It's in those moments that real creativity is born. This personal encouragement diary gives you permission to hurt, heal and rejoice. Using powerful imagery and prose, Amanda awakens you to your purpose and takes you on an adventure where you explore and unleash the genius that is you.

Fadzi Whande
Award-winning Global Diversity and Inclusion Strategist and Social Justice Advocate

This book will not only inspire you to activate your creativity but will challenge the limits that you may or may not know that you narrate over your life. These pages are honest and can help anyone discover more about their deeper levels of creativity. If any person completely indulges themselves and commits to mulling over each "sphere of the creative process", you will not only discover fruit but your creative potential.

Matt Myers
Creative Pastor, Hillsong Perth

Amanda has a beautiful way of drawing authenticity out of others and sharing her vulnerability with grace and courage. Reading her work is like sitting with a dear friend and talking over coffee. You come away feeling challenged and empowered.

Lizzy Milani
Writer, Speaker and Co-founder The Practice Co

Amanda Viviers', "Dear Creative Self" is a must for a creative in any sphere. Through honestly sharing the ups and downs in her own creative journey, Amanda encourages others in theirs. The mix of memoir, reflection, and practical application is perfect for a creative at any stage on their journey.

Amanda's wisdom is born from many years of leading and growing in the area of creativity. Her voice of encouragement is needed in this area, that is often rife with competition and comparison.

Do your creative self a favour and pick up her book today!

Jodie McCarthy
Writer, Speaker and Poet

ENDORSEMENTS

Amanda writes to unleash her readers from the ties of their inner critic and to introduce them to their true and brave selves. This book will transform you in the best way possible.

Dr Rebecca Ray
Author, Clinical Psychologist and Speaker

I have had the pleasure of working with Amanda in different work settings for over twenty years. Her creative mind, entrepreneurship and energy are infectious and inspiring and helps instil a culture of 'can-do' and 'anything is possible'. Her positive energy and enthusiasm calls individuals and teams to new ways of thinking and innovating. She is relentlessly inspirational.

Penny Webb
Co-founder of Kinwomen, CEO, Author and Speaker

This might be the most useful book a creative could ever read. Not because it is a step by step guide to writing, but because Amanda shows you how to find gold in the smallest of places. If you ever wanted to get off the sidelines and back-yourself in the creative game, then Dear Creative Self is your new platform. This work is a result of Amanda's practical talents and deep insight that will guide its readers into a genuine expression of the heart's call to creativity. You will learn that to access the natural and spiritual parts of the self, being creative demands constructive solitude to open an expanse of artistic independence.

I have found Amanda to be one who champions the authentic voice of every person she meets. Through her experience of a negative story, Amanda totally owns the gift of encouraging others to write and, when necessary, re-write their own story. I enjoy Amanda's remarkable character trait of humility that allows her to unveil her journey in a spiritually inspiring way. From birthing an idea to unlocking the blocks that stop us from living a wild adventure, Amanda will show you that you DO have what it takes to be a unique, successful creative. Amanda's most famous quote "Someone Needs Your Story" speaks of the urgency of your creative gift to the world. So when should you read this? The time is right now.

Anne Galambosi
Clinical Psychologist, Author, Speaker and Pastor

Dear creative self is a retreat for your soul to breathe, explore and rise. It is a space to sink deep into the connection we all are searching for in unearthing our purpose, our life rhythm and our faith. Amanda's gift is in curating a space for each of us to courageously express our stories and creative dreams. She is, at the core, a champion of people's hearts, passions and divine gifts.

Mish Pope
Coach & Speaker

DEAR CREATIVE SELF

With this new gift of a book, my dear friend Amanda welcomes us into her heart and her story with every authentic word in every vulnerable letter on every transparent page. And in doing so, she gives us our own permission slip to choose to join her; to enter into our own stories with wild hearts, honesty, bravery, guts and kindness. To dive deep, choose adventure, search well, breathe fully, have fun, write to explore, create again and become your true creative self.

I'm in, I'm all in. It's time. Thank you dear heart.

Bronwen Healy
Author, Speaker, Founder

Amanda's writing is unique, fresh and speaks straight into the hearts of those who read and share her books. Personally, I have been reading Amanda's books for over 10 years and had the privilege of listening to her speak on many occasions.

Over my career, I have read thousands of books on self and professional development, and her style is truly authentic and genuine.

Donna Bates
Strategic Advisor & Leadership Mentor. Internationally Accredited John Maxwell Leadership Speaker & Coach

Our Creative Selves need to be mobilized like an army waging war on the darkness. Each word of "Dear Creative Self" awakened something dormant in my heart, in my soul, deep within the very fibre of my being.

And I wept

And I smiled

And I was challenged (since I was reading at 4:30 am because I woke and couldn't sleep and then read your chapter on sleep!)

But oh, was it worth it!

As a pioneer and church planter, it reminds me to continue advancing the mission and drawing on the creative courage it takes to break open a city. As a coach and counsellor, it reminds me that there is healing for our creative souls, and creativity can be part of healing our souls. With Amanda's insight, I broke the power of this lie years and years ago, when I first read her early books.

This book will do the same! It will release people into the power of creativity and its potential for your life.

Vanessa Hoyes
Pastor, Coach and Counsellor in Canada

ENDORSEMENTS

Dear creative soul, Amanda Viviers' new book, is for you. Amanda is a creative entrepreneur of the best kind-she lives and breathes what she teaches and will inspire you to feed and foster your creative self.

She will help you to explore your creativity in deeper, mystical, and more practical ways than you've ever done before. If you've read Amanda's previous books, participated in one of her workshops or sat in one of her keynotes, you'll know what I mean.

Amanda shares the delights of a butterfly landing on her nose in the sea, the beauty of routines shaped by grace, the benefits of a procrastination-busting basketful of unfinished projects and the joy of the sacred secret spaces in our souls.

This book speaks to your creative self in such a way that it will not only stand up and listen, but it will also sing, and soar, and shoot for the stars.

This is not a how-to book, it's a me-too book. As Amanda shares her creative journey in her quintessential vulnerable style, your creative self will want what she's having.

Elaine Fraser
Writer and mentor for emerging writers. Author of five books including, Beautiful and Too Beautiful

Dear Creative Self,
Buy the book!
Sincerely,
You

Tucked into the shadow laden spaces of your being, there is a small whisper from something so extraordinary. It is patiently waiting for you to call it forth. Amidst the noise of social media and constant push to create more and produce on-demand, there lies a perfectly imperfect piece of yourself that is gently reminding you of its very existence. Through Amanda's stories, letters, and inspirational exercises you will find the permission you need to embrace your creative self, heal from past stories, and begin the process of creating in a way that is unique life-giving to you.

Dear Creative Self Isn't merely for the poets and artist, but rather the created. Through creation, we came into being, and since we were born with creativity, it is through creativity, we find our true self. It has been said that there are two great days in our life, the moment we are born, and the moment we realise why we are here. Life is short, and with each turn of the pages of this book, you will find the greatest story you will ever read, the one you write for yourself. It's time to free your creative self.

Diana Henderson
Photographer, Author, and Speaker

www.ingramcontent.com/pod-product-compliance
Lightning Source LLC
LaVergne TN
LVHW011833060526
838200LV00053B/4002